A LETTER FROM PETER MUNK

Since we started the Munk Debates, my wife, Melanie, and I have been deeply gratified at how quickly they have captured the public's imagination. From the time of our first event in May 2008, we have hosted what I believe are some of the most exciting public policy debates in Canada and internationally. Global in focus, the Munk Debates have tackled a range of issues, such as humanitarian intervention, the effectiveness of foreign aid, the threat of global warming, religion's impact on geopolitics, the rise of China, and the decline of Europe. These compelling topics have served as intellectual and ethical grist for some of the world's most important thinkers and doers, from Henry Kissinger to Tony Blair, Christopher Hitchens to Paul Krugman, Peter Mandelson to Fareed Zakaria.

The issues raised at the Munk Debates have not only fostered public awareness, but they have also helped many of us become more involved and, therefore, less intimidated by the concept of globalization. It is so easy to be inward-looking. It is so easy to be xenophobic. It is so easy to be nationalistic. It is hard to go into the unknown. Globalization, for many people, is an abstract concept at best. The purpose of this debate series is to help people feel more familiar with our fast-changing world and more comfortable participating in the universal dialogue about the issues and events that will shape our collective future.

I don't need to tell you that that there are many, many burning issues. Global warming, the plight of extreme poverty, genocide, or our shaky financial order: these are just a few of the critical issues that matter to people. And it seems to me, and to my foundation board members, that the quality of the public dialogue on these critical issues diminishes in direct proportion to the salience and number of these issues clamouring for our attention. By trying to highlight the most important issues at crucial moments in the global conversation, these debates not only profile the ideas and opinions of some of the world's brightest thinkers, but they also crystallize public passion and knowledge, helping to tackle some of the challenges confronting humankind.

I have learned in life — and I'm sure many of you will share this view — that challenges bring out the best in us. I hope you'll agree that the participants in these debates challenge not only each other but also each of us to think clearly and logically about important problems facing our world.

Peter Munk
Founder, Aurea Foundation
Toronto, Ontario

SHOULD THE WEST ENGAGE PUTIN'S RUSSIA?

POZNER AND COHEN VS. APPLEBAUM AND KASPAROV

THE MUNK DEBATES

Edited by Rudyard Griffiths

ANANSI

This edition published in 2015 by
House of Anansi Press Inc.
110 Spadina Avenue, Suite 801
Toronto, ON, M5V 2K4
Tel. 416-363-4343
Fax 416-363-1017
www.houseofanansi.com

House of Anansi Press is committed to protecting our natural environment.
As part of our efforts, the interior of this book is printed on paper that contains
100% post-consumer recycled fibres, is acid-free, and is processed chlorine-free.

19 18 17 16 15   1 2 3 4 5

Library and Archives Canada Cataloguing in Publication

Should the West engage Putin's Russia? / by Stephen F.
Cohen and Vladimir Pozner (pro) vs. Anne Applebaum and
Garry Kasparov (con); edited by Rudyard Griffiths.

(The Munk debates)
Issued in print and electronic formats.
ISBN: 978-1-77089-858-5 (paperback). ISBN: 978-1-77089-859-2 (html).

1. Russia (Federation) — Foreign relations —Western countries.
2. Western countries — Foreign relations — Russia (Federation).
3. Sanctions (International law).
I. Cohen, Stephen F., panelist II. Kasparov, G. K. (Garri Kimovich), panelist
III. Pozner, Vladimir, panelist IV. Applebaum, Anne, 1964–, panelist
V. Griffiths, Rudyard, editor VI. Series: Munk debates

JZ1616.A5S56 2015   327.470182'1   C2015-904735-8
                           C2015-904736-6

Library of Congress Control Number: 2015944670

Cover design: Alysia Shewchuk
Transcription: Rondi Adamson

*We acknowledge for their financial support of our publishing program
the Canada Council for the Arts, the Ontario Arts Council, and the Government of
Canada through the Canada Book Fund.*

Printed and bound in Canada

MIX
Paper from
responsible sources
FSC® C004071

CONTENTS

It is the geopolitical debate of the moment: How should the West respond to the actions of Vladimir Putin's Russia? For some the answer is obvious. Russia's annexation of Crimea and its waging of a "hybrid war" in eastern Ukraine that has left over 6,000 people dead and another 16,000 wounded demands a concerted and forceful international response. Russia should be subjected to crippling economic sanctions targeting not just Putin and his inner circle but the country's banking, energy, and industrial sectors. Russia should be kicked out of the West-led international institutions that had previously welcomed Russian participation. The embattled Ukrainian military should be supplied with lethal defensive weapons to target separatist artillery and mortars. The North Atlantic Treaty Organization (NATO) should deploy troops to the Baltic States and threaten the use of military force if Russia tries to violate the sovereignty of a NATO member state. In short, Russia should be made to pay an ongoing and punishing price for its actions in Crimea and Ukraine — one steep enough to convince Putin to halt the destabilization of eastern Ukraine and forgo any ambitions he might have to empower Russian minorities in other former Soviet republics. Isolation, not engagement, is the only strategy to contain Russia.

But is taking a hard line on Russia going to further peace and stability in eastern Europe, or the West's own geopolitical interests? Like any conflict, the origins of the current standoff between Russia and the West are complex and multi-faceted. Since the end of the Cold War, the West has needlessly stoked Russian anxieties about encirclement and regime change by aggressively expanding NATO into the former Soviet bloc. The West's disregard for Russia's "sphere of influence" is why Putin ultimately reacted the way he did to the ousting of Ukraine's pro-Russian government and the installation of a pro-European parliament in Kiev. The conflict in Ukraine isn't as simple as a good versus bad struggle between European reformers and Russian-backed Ukrainian oligarchs. This is a nation deeply divided by history, religion, and ethnicity, and Russia has legitimate concerns about the security of Russian minorities in Crimea and eastern Ukraine. By isolating Putin, the West threatens vital security interests it shares with Russia — from Syria to Iran to the balance of power in Asia — thereby increasing the risks for global instability and conflict.

These were the sharp and compelling battle lines at the Munk Debate on Russia, which was attended by over

3,000 people in Toronto, Canada, in April 2015. Four outstanding debaters took the stage to debate the motion "Be it resolved the West should engage not isolate Russia." Garry Kasparov — Russian-born political dissident, outspoken critic of Vladimir Putin, and the world's greatest living chess player — argued against the resolution. Kasparov was joined on stage by Anne Applebaum, an internationally renowned expert on Russian history, a director at the prestigious Legatum Institute on global affairs in London, and the Pulitzer Prize–winning author of *Gulag: A History.*

Vladimir Pozner and Stephen F. Cohen were their opponents in the debate, tasked with making the case for engaging Russia. Pozner is a veteran Russian journalist, a bestselling author who has been called the "Voice of Moscow" by CNN, and is the host of the top-rated weekly current affairs program on Russia's largest television network. Stephen F. Cohen is a vocal American proponent of Russian engagement with the West. Cohen is a professor emeritus of history and Russian studies at New York University and has advised former Soviet president Mikhail Gorbachev and former U.S. president George H.W. Bush on East-West relations.

Neither team of debaters yielded a single point or argument, from the debate's opening remarks to its last on-stage pronouncements. Vladimir Pozner set the hard-fought tone of the evening when he argued that the West should acknowledge the role its post–Cold War policy toward Russia played in creating the current crisis. Pozner bluntly characterized the West's policy as "You lost the

Cold War and you'll pay for it. Just shut up. Go back into your cave. You're a second-rate country and we don't care about you anymore." He went on, "Russia today would be a very different country had the West — the United States first and foremost — decided to engage Gorbachev's Soviet Union and then Yeltsin's Russia with the same aims with which it engaged post–World War II Germany and Italy, to help create and support democratic development and institutions."

The acerbic Anne Applebaum rejected outright any analysis that sought to blame Western actions toward Russia for the current crisis: "To be clear, the Russia we have today is the result of our failed policy of engagement. Have we isolated and humiliated Russia since 1991? I would say no. Post-Soviet Russia was not humiliated and was given *de facto* great power status, as you've just heard. Russia received the Soviet United Nations (UN) seat, and the Soviet embassies and nuclear weapons, which were transferred from Ukraine... Since the fall of the Soviet Union, a series of American presidents, all of them, in fact, have sought to build up Russia's international status."

Throughout the debate Stephen F. Cohen repeatedly hammered home the idea that adopting a policy of isolation toward Russia would undermine the West's interests: "Ukraine has already cost us in terms of our national security. We have lost a security partner in the Kremlin, not just Putin, but perhaps for generations or, at least, years to come. It is splitting Europe against American leadership and possibly undermining the transatlantic alliance and plunging us into a new Cold War. It is bringing us closer to an actual war with nuclear Russia than we have been since the Cuban Missile Crisis. These are the facts."

Garry Kasparov's many contributions to the debate focused on Putin and how his status as an all-powerful leader made him a dangerous and unpredictable opponent who would only respond to isolation. In Kasparov's opinion as a keen observer of Russian politics: "If Putin is not stopped in Ukraine, he will continue to move further outside of Russia. He will start provocations in the Baltic countries in order to undermine NATO because he needs chaos and muddy waters. That is the way for him to survive politically. It is all about domestic politics, because he has nothing else to offer besides foreign policy expansion."

These statements by four outstanding debaters provide a snapshot of what was a rich, sophisticated, and fiercely argued debate that ranged over topics as varied as the future of Russian democracy, the evolution of "hybrid wars" as a new and dangerous international phenomenon, and the existential dangers of atomic weapons in conflicts that involve nuclear powers such as Russia.

The Munk Debate on Russia deservedly stands out of one of the series most successful contests to date. We hope readers enjoy the debate transcribed here in its entirety with additional commentary and analysis by each of the four debaters.

Rudyard Griffiths,
Chair, The Munk Debates
Toronto, May 2015

Should the West Engage Putin's Russia?

Pro: Vladimir Pozner and Stephen F. Cohen
Con: Anne Applebaum and Garry Kasparov

April 10, 2015
Toronto, Ontario

SHOULD THE WEST ENGAGE PUTIN'S RUSSIA?

RUDYARD GRIFFITHS: Ladies and gentlemen, welcome. My name is Rudyard Griffiths and it is my privilege to both organize this debate series and to serve as your moderator. I want to start tonight's proceedings by welcoming the North American–wide radio and television audience tuning into this debate everywhere from CBC Radio's *Ideas* to CPAC, Canada's Public Affairs Channel, to C-SPAN, across the continental United States. A warm hello also to our online audience, watching right now on munkdebates.com; it's terrific to have you as virtual participants tonight. And finally, I'd like to welcome the over 3,000 people that have filled Roy Thomson Hall to capacity for another Munk Debate.

Tonight represents a milestone for the Munk Debates: this is our fifteenth semi-annual event. We've been at this for seven-and-a-half years, and our ability to bring the brightest minds and the sharpest thinkers here to Toronto to debate the big issues facing the world and Canada would not be possible without the foresight, generosity, and commitment of our series hosts. Ladies and gentlemen, please join me in an appreciation for the co-founders of the Aurea Foundation, Peter and Melanie Munk.

Let's get this debate underway and our debaters out here on centre stage. Arguing for the resolution, "Be it resolved the West should engage not isolate Russia," is the Emmy Award–winning journalist, top-rated Russian TV broadcaster and bestselling author Vladimir Pozner. Pozner's teammate tonight is Stephen F. Cohen, a celebrated scholar of Soviet and post-Soviet Russia and a contributing editor at *The Nation* magazine, who's here from New York City.

One team of great debaters deserves another and arguing against the resolution is the Warsaw-based, Pulitzer Prize–winning author and *Washington Post* columnist Anne Applebaum. Anne's debating partner tonight is Garry Kasparov, the prominent Russian dissident and chair of the New York–based Human Rights Foundation. He is, however, probably best known as the world's greatest living chess player.

Before we call on our debaters for their opening remarks, I need to go over one housekeeping point: our countdown clock. This clock will appear on the screen at various times during tonight's debate, including for opening and closing statements, and for timed rebuttals. When you see it count down to zero, please join me in a round of applause. This is going to keep our speakers on their toes, and our debate on schedule.

Let's review how the audience voted on tonight's resolution before this debate. You were asked, "The West should engage not isolate Russia." Interesting results: 58 percent agree with the motion and 42 percent disagree. This debate could really go either way. And to get a sense of how much of public opinion is in play tonight we asked you a second question: Are you open to changing your vote depending on what you hear during this debate? We have an indecisive audience: 86 percent of you could go either way. So, things are very much in play.

Let's welcome all the debaters to the stage.

We agreed beforehand to the order of opening statements. Vladimir Pozner, your six minutes start now.

VLADIMIR POZNER: Ladies and gentlemen, I have not come here to argue Russia's case. I have come here to argue the case that isolating any country is not only counterproductive but dangerous, especially if the country is as big, as wealthy, as powerful, and as unpredictable as Russia.

Allow me to share with all of you a bit of history: When the Russian Empire crumbled in 1917 and the Bolsheviks came to power, the West refused to recognize first Soviet Russia and then the Soviet Union. Isolation and non-engagement were the words of the day, and so, for about a decade, the country was portrayed as an evil power by the Western media and left to stew in its own juices. The prediction was that it would inevitably fall

3

apart—that it was economically dead in the water—and that its people would rise up and destroy the regime.

As we all know, none of this happened. In 1929, the West was hit by the worst economic crisis in its history. Meanwhile, in 1929, the U.S.S.R. announced its first five-year plan of economic development. Over those years of non-recognition and isolation, the Stalin-led Soviet leadership conducted a massive bloodbath throughout the country: it physically wiped out all political opposition; destroyed millions and millions of peasants who had refused to adhere to the collective farm system; and starved to death millions of Ukrainian farmers who would not bow to the draconian demands for wheat and flour. It was in the process of annihilating Russia's most precious human resource, the intelligentsia, and was in the process of creating a new human entity, the so-called *Homo Sovieticus*. The Great Terror of 1937 and 1938 lay just ahead.

The West's policy of non-recognition, non-engagement, and isolation—non-interference, if you will—and the absence of any united outcry, all played a role in allowing the Soviet system to evolve the way it did.

It would be remiss of me, on the eve of the seventieth anniversary of the defeat of Nazi Germany, not to mention the fact that by the end of the 1930s, the West—in particular Great Britain and France—refused to engage the U.S.S.R. in an alliance against Hitler. The consequence was the infamous Molotov-Ribbentrop Pact of August 1939 between Hitler and Stalin that contained a secret protocol that sold off the independent Baltic states of Estonia, Latvia, and Lithuania, as well as a part of Poland, to the Soviet Union in exchange for a commitment to non-aggression between the two countries.

And while it was ultimately the Soviet Union that broke the Nazis' back — a fact confirmed by the likes of Winston Churchill and Franklin Delano Roosevelt — it is also true that the Soviet Union went on to occupy all the countries of eastern Europe as well as some of central Europe. It is also true that the country became a military superpower, and we should thank our lucky stars that World War III never happened, thanks to mutually assured destruction (MAD).

The U.S.S.R. did not fall apart because it was isolated, or because of non-engagement on the part of the West, which in fact made it stronger. The U.S.S.R. fell apart because the system ceased to function. It was simply not viable. And what was the West's response when Gorbachev and then Yeltsin came to power? Did the West engage the new Russia?

If we look a little bit beyond the good old Gorby-era PR spiel that was spewed out by the West for popular consumption, the policy was essentially: You lost the Cold War and you'll pay for it. Just shut up. Go back into your cave. You're a second-rate country and we don't care about you anymore.

Russia today would be a very different country had the West — the United States first and foremost — decided to engage Gorbachev's Soviet Union and then Yeltsin's Russia with the same aims with which it engaged post–World War II Germany and Italy, to help create and support democratic development and institutions.

In conclusion, the Russia that exists today is to a large extent the result of non-engagement by the West, of a policy aimed at humbling what is a nation of proud people. I vote for engagement because I want to see change in Russia, positive change both for Russia and for the West. Thank you.

RUDYARD GRIFFITHS: Anne Applebaum, you're up next.

ANNE APPLEBAUM: Thank you, Rudyard, and thank you to this fantastic audience, but no thanks to whoever wrote the resolution that Garry Kasparov and I must oppose this evening. I, like the rest of you, believe very strongly that engagement is a positive thing. Engagement, integration, peace, and prosperity are all linked. Isolation, by contrast, sounds negative and confrontational.

I have been a long-time advocate for the integration of eastern Europe with the West, and initially I believed that engagement, which works so brilliantly in Poland, where I live, could work for Russia, too. Alas, I have concluded, after long experience, that for the moment it can't — because this current Russian regime, as it now exists, cannot be engaged.

Putin's Russia is not just another autocracy or traditional Russian dictatorship, as Stephen F. Cohen will probably tell you. Russia's current leaders are not simply the political rulers of their nation. They are literally the country's owners: they control all of its major companies, all of its media, and all of its natural wealth. During the 1990s they took over the Russian state, in league with organized crime, using theft, graft, and money laundering.

As a result, Russia is one of the most unequal countries in the world, with 110 Russians controlling 35 percent of the nation's wealth. Many of those people also work in or with the Kremlin.

Whatever you want to call this system—a mafia state, a feudal empire—it's a disaster for ordinary Russians, but it is also extremely dangerous for everybody else. In order to stay in power and to keep this tiny group of people enriched, Putin and his cronies have long needed not only to spread the system to their immediate neighbours but to undermine rule of law and democracy in the West as well.

How does this work? Putin and his henchmen badly need to keep the international financial system safe for corrupt money. To do so, they buy Western politicians. For example, when in power, former German chancellor Gerhard Schröder stopped an investigation into a financial scam closely connected to Putin. Schröder now works for Gazprom, the Russian energy company.

Putin's cronies have also invested heavily in strategically important European companies, hoping that by doing so they'll acquire the political influence they need to protect their dishonest schemes. They make ample use of tax havens, thereby enriching the providers of these corruption services and depriving legitimate governments of revenue. How do we stop this? Only by disengaging and isolating the problem. Let's get Russian money out of the Western financial system.

A second example: Putin and his henchmen are often frustrated by Western multilateral institutions, such as the

European Union (EU) and NATO. A united EU energy policy would make it much more difficult for Russia to use its gas pipelines the way it does now—to blackmail and bully its neighbours. If it weren't for NATO, Russia would find it much easier, for example, to take the land that it badly wants in the Arctic. And so the Russian regime has invested heavily in anti-European, anti-transatlantic, and even fascist political movements all across Europe.

A Russian bank has lent nine million euros to Marine Le Pen, the leader of the far right in France. Russia also maintains strong political and financial links to the anti-Semitic Jobbik party in Hungary and to far-right groups in Germany, Italy, and many other countries. What to do about this problem? We need to disengage and we need to isolate. Let's get Russian money out of European politics.

A third example: the Russian regime has invested massively in an enormous system of disinformation—television stations in multiple languages, web sites, fake think-tanks, a vast army of Internet trolls—whose work is now well documented, and which are designed to create chaos and confusion. This isn't traditional propaganda. It's not about saying that Russia is a great country.

When a Russian missile shot down a Malaysian plane over eastern Ukraine last summer, the Russian media responded with multiple absurd conspiracy theories, including that the plane was full of dead people when it took off. But even on an ordinary day, Russia Today, the Russian English-language TV station, has reported on the Central Intelligence Agency's (CIA's) invention of Ebola. The point of these stories is to create a fog of disinformation so that no one knows what is true and what is not anymore. How can we break through this fog and shore up our traditions of objective reporting? We have to disengage and isolate. Let's work harder to identify Russian lies and get them out of our media.

You'll note that I haven't yet mentioned Ukraine, which is because I believe you can't understand the recent crisis there until you understand the true nature of the current Russian regime. For two decades now, Russia has maintained control over Ukraine by investing in politicians, companies, and disinformation. Putin hoped to create a Ukraine with a copycat, colonial version of the political system he invented in Russia — and he almost succeeded. The young pro-European and pro-democracy Ukrainians, who protested on the streets in December 2013, were not fighting Russia as a nation. They were fighting oligarchs, corruption, and Putinism. How can we assist these young Ukrainians?

I repeat: we need to disengage and to isolate Putinist Russia. We need to maintain sanctions on Putin's cronies, those 110 people around him who control their country. We need to make Putin pay a high price for invading a neighbour so that he doesn't invade another one. And the best way to do this is to isolate Russian money, isolate Russian oligarchs, malign Russian political influence and propaganda, and prevent Russian violence and corruption from distorting the politics of Europe and North America. Putinism is a danger to Russians, to Ukrainians, and to all of us. Thank you very much.

RUDYARD GRIFFITHS: You finished with ten seconds on the clock, Anne. Impressive. Stephen, you're up next.

STEPHEN F. COHEN: Unlike Ms. Applebaum, I come here, my first trip to Canada, as a patriot of American and Canadian security, on behalf of my family, and yours. I believe that we need a partner in the Kremlin if we are going to have global security — not a friend, but a partner who shares our fundamental security interest. To achieve that, we must not merely engage Russia; we must pursue full co-operation on security and other matters. National security, for both Canada and the U.S., still runs through Moscow. This is an existential truth.

I want you to consider something I'm going to share over the course of this debate. Remember what the former United States senator Daniel Patrick Moynihan once said: "Everyone is entitled to his or her own opinions, but not to his or her own facts." It's profound.

Here are the facts: The world today is much more dangerous, far less stable and ordered than it was twenty-five years ago when the Soviet Union existed. There are more nuclear states but less control over the sale of nuclear weapons, over nuclear know-how, and over nuclear material. There are more regional conflicts, more open ethnic and religious hatreds, and there is more political extremism and intolerance. As a result, there is more terrorism in more places.

And to make matters worse, there is more economic and social deprivation and resentment. And as we all know, there are more environmental dangers and foreseeable shortages of the earth's resources.

Here's the other fact: not one of these existential dangers can be dealt with effectively without Russia's cooperation, no matter who sits in the Kremlin. Even after the fall of the Soviet Union, Russia remains the world's largest territorial country, and one that straddles the fateful frontline between Western and Islamic civilization. Russia still has, proportionately, more of the world's natural resources, from energy to freshwater, than any other nation.

And, of course, Russia has its arsenals and stockpiles of every conceivable weapon of mass destruction. Whether we like it or not, Russia still has sympathizers, partners, and allies around the world, even in Europe and the Western hemisphere. These are facts. Not opinions.

What is the alternative? Our opponents say it is to isolate Russia. They want to weaken, destabilize, and carry out regime change — as if it were that easy — in Russia. They rely not on facts but on three fundamental fallacies based on their opinions.

Fallacy #1: In this globalized world, it is impossible to isolate Russia. Russia is too big, too rich, too interconnected. Russia has many options, apart from the West. Ever since President Obama said, several months ago, that it was American policy to isolate Russia, the Russian state, under Putin, has signed more financial, political, economic, and military agreements with foreign states than Washington. Russia is connected. Russia has other places to go if we push it out of the West.

Fallacy #2: Isolating Russia from the West will not make Moscow more co-operative or compliant. Instead, we know what Russia will do—it's already doing it. It will turn elsewhere, above all to China, and to many other regions and regimes around the world that harbour resentments against America, Europe, and Canada. And what will Russia do if we so isolate it? It will sell these countries nuclear reactors—excellent weapons. It will give them credit, and it will protect them politically at the United Nations with its veto.

Fallacy #3: A weakened, destabilized Russia will make every danger I have listed worse and create new ones. Consider, for example, if this policy of isolation, with its sub-policy of weakening Moscow, were to succeed. What would become of Russia's weapons of mass destruction if Moscow's control over them diminished? Think about that and yourselves. Think about your children. Think about this kind of madness. Is that what we really want?

Finally, what are the fundamental arguments our opponents make in favour of trying to isolate Russia? They make none that I can see. The towering example, and one which I knew Ms. Applebaum would mention, is Ukraine. What happened in Ukraine is entirely Putin's fault. The West bears no responsibility: we made no mistakes in our policy whatsoever. This is not factual.

I want to conclude by pointing out what Ukraine has already cost us in terms of our national security. We have lost a security partner in the Kremlin, not just Putin, but perhaps for generations or, at least, years to come. It is splitting Europe against American leadership and possibly undermining the transatlantic alliance and plunging us into a new Cold War. It is bringing us closer to an actual war with nuclear Russia than we have been since the Cuban Missile Crisis. These are the facts.

RUDYARD GRIFFITHS: Thank you, Stephen. Garry Kasparov, you have six minutes.

GARRY KASPAROV: Thank you very much. I'm here not as just a neighbour of Mr. Cohen, because we both live on the Upper West Side of New York, but as a patriot of my country, Russia.

I don't feel very comfortable arguing against the resolution. My dream when I was a kid, as a chess prodigy travelling abroad, playing under the Soviet and eventually under the Russian flag, was to help make my country a real factor in the progress of humanity. I knew that despite the regime that I hated — the Soviet Union at that time — that Russia had huge intellectual and cultural potential, and that it also had natural resources.

It seemed to me, and to millions of others in my country and in eastern Europe, that our dream had come true in 1991. The regime collapsed, and we all remember the celebrating crowds, pulling down the statue of KGB founder Felix Dzerzhinsky, and the talk of purification and escaping from a cage. It was not an easy time; Yugoslavia had also collapsed and then it fell into a terrible civil war. Russia happily escaped that, thanks to Boris Yeltsin and his wisdom and ability to understand that we needed an agreement with the former Soviet republics.

Russia was engaged from the very beginning. What about all the billions and billions of Western money given as aid to support Russia's economy? And in 1998, during the financial crisis, it was an International Monetary Fund (IMF) loan that actually helped Russia to escape from the abyss. By the end of Yeltsin's rule Russia was already on the verge of recovery. Actually, the highest growth of gross domestic product (GDP) in Russia was in the year 2000. And then Putin came to power. The greatest mistake Yeltsin made was to hand over power to a KGB lieutenant colonel nine years after the collapse of the Soviet Union.

And what was the first thing Putin did? He restored the Soviet anthem for those who had ears to hear his long-term agenda. And we began to see the total collapse of the feeble democracy created under Yeltsin. First, the country became a one-party dictatorship, and then it became a one-man dictatorship, the most unstable and dangerous form of government. The whole legacy of the regime is based on his charisma and his ability to excite the audience — the entire propaganda machine works for his greatness. And again, we know from history that after running out of enemies inside a country, these dictators turn elsewhere.

In 2005, I stopped playing chess and I turned toward what some people have mistakenly called Russian politics. I say that because when you traditionally think of politics you think about political parties, debates, fundraising, and elections. Russia has no live television or public debates.

So I knew it would be an uphill battle, one in which my chess experience couldn't help me at all. In chess we have fixed rules and unpredictable results. Putin's Russia is the exact the opposite. And all of this has happened during the West's engagement with the country. I remember watching with horror while Putin hosted the G7 in 2006. I never called it G8, by the way, because for me it was always G7 plus one.

Russian inclusion in the G8 was essentially given to Yeltsin as an advance, like a preliminary reward. Russia was not a democracy and it was not a great industrial power. China never made it into the G8 and neither did India, but Russia did. And how could we attack Putin and his democratic values if we watched him being embraced by Bush, Blair, Berlusconi, and Chirac? The Russian propaganda machine used this to Putin's advantage.

And while we are talking about foreign aggression, I can't avoid mentioning the issue of Ukraine. The Russian invasion of Ukraine undermines the authority of NATO and the United States. And it was the only thing Putin could do to maintain his grip on power. The economy alone could no longer sustain his reign.

He has become a ruler for life, and everybody seems to understand it. He needed to invade Ukraine for the same reasons he invaded Georgia in 2008. And let's not forget that Ukraine was disarmed by the United States and the United Kingdom in 1994, when it was forced to sign the Budapest Memorandum. Few people in this audience know that at that time, Ukraine had the third largest nuclear arsenal in the world — more than the U.K., France, and China combined. Ukraine had 1,200 nuclear warheads. If some of these warheads were aimed at Moscow today, Putin would never have crossed the

Ukrainian border. That document, which included the signatures of Bill Clinton and John Major, also disarmed small nuclear arsenals from Kazakhstan and Belarus. It created a nuclear-free former Soviet Union, but it was done in exchange for territorial integrity.

And if you think that Crimea is a regional, local problem, you're wrong. The message being sent to every country in the world is that if you want to protect your sovereignty, get some nukes, which is why the Ukrainian crisis affects everybody on this planet. I don't want to isolate Russia; I want to isolate Putin's regime, which is a dangerous virus. You don't engage a virus. It needs to be contained. Contamination is not the answer. Thank you.

RUDYARD GRIFFITHS: Great opening statements. Now, we're going to move on to timed rebuttals. We want to give each side an opportunity to rebut what they have heard so far. The pro side will speak first. Vladimir, you've got two minutes.

VLADIMIR POZNER: If we're going to be honest, the majority of people in this audience really don't know much about Russia or Ukraine. And so the debaters up on stage can really say anything. Billions and billions of dollars were not invested in Russia. You've got to be kidding me. And whatever was invested was invested to make money.

And as for Putin's supposed cronies, why are they called "cronies"? Why are they not his comrades? We're debating semantics and not facts.

Here are the facts: if Ukraine had nuclear missiles, can you imagine what kind of a chess game we'd have? There would be nobody left to play it. Is that what we're looking for? We should be thankful they don't have missiles in that country. The fewer missiles there are in the world, the better. Do we want a Russia that is pushed out of everything, doing whatever it wants, and in no way answering for its actions? A country that is not under any pressure from the outside world because it's not engaged? Or do we want a policy of engagement?

Russia has always been in the crosshairs of the West, and perhaps for good reason. So if you think this is just a Putin issue, you've made a big mistake. It's about a much more basic relationship.

STEPHEN F. COHEN: I didn't know that Mr. Kasparov was stalking me. I had no idea he lived on the Upper West Side. And I'm hoping we'll end up in a coffee shop there for a friendly talk. But I wouldn't want him making any Western policy.

Henry Kissinger, who is ninety-one and not thought to be soft on anybody, wrote in Ms. Applebaum's own newspaper back in March 2014 that "the demonization of Vladimir Putin is not a policy; it's an alibi for the absence of one." I would say that Dr. Kissinger could have gone further and said that the demonization of Putin is an excuse to abandon analysis, to obscure perilous facts, and to make statements about an evil in Moscow—that it's a mafia state—and to compare Putin to Hitler. This approach is wrong.

Alongside this line of thinking inevitably comes this romance of the Yeltsin 'nineties. Maybe it was great time for Mr. Kasparov. Maybe it was beneficial to Poland and eastern Europe. I don't know. But when Mr. Yeltsin was forced from office, 75 percent of Russians lived in poverty, as Garry well knows. The billions and billions of American and Western dollars they so romantically think were sent to Moscow were collected by Mr. Yeltsin's friends and sent back to the Bank of New York, where they were laundered — a criminal case was brought against the bank for that later. So this romantic idea of the 1990s is completely deceptive. Russia was on its knees, ruled by a weak ruler and pillaged by a mafia. So let's think about the real problems in the world, and about our security, please.

RUDYARD GRIFFITHS: Anne?

ANNE APPLEBAUM: To be clear, the Russia we have today is the result of our failed policy of engagement. Have we isolated and humiliated Russia since 1991? I would say no. Post-Soviet Russia was not humiliated and was given *de facto* great power status, as you've just heard. Russia received the Soviet UN seat, and the Soviet embassies and nuclear weapons, which were transferred from Ukraine under the terms of the 1994 Budapest Memorandum. Since the fall of the Soviet Union, a series of American presidents — all of them, in fact — have sought to build up Russia's international status.

Presidents Clinton and Bush invited Russia to join the G8, even though Russia was not one of the world's top economies. Russia was invited to join the Council of Europe, although it is not a democracy. Russia was invited to join the World Trade Organization (WTO), whose rules it systematically violates.

What was Russia doing during this same period, while we were engaging and inviting the country into our institutions? Putin invaded Chechnya, not once but twice. He invaded Georgia. He invaded Ukraine. He built up his military system.

Last month he held a military exercise in the Arctic, involving 80,000 troops, 220 aircraft, and 41 ships. Earlier this year he conducted an equally vast exercise in the Baltic. In 2009 and in 2013 he conducted military exercises, which concluded with a practice run of a nuclear bombardment of Warsaw.

You can't have it both ways. You can't say Putin was laundering his money in Western banks and that we were isolating him. What was Russia doing while we let it utilize our banking system and enrich itself? It was recreating a Soviet-style nuclear arsenal and a Soviet-style military to use against us.

GARRY KASPAROV: I am always willing to learn, but this is the first time I've heard someone suggest that a policy of engagement in the 1920s could have prevented Stalinist terror. I always believed that it was a criminal regime founded by Lenin and Stalin among others, and that whatever the West did in the 1920s was irrelevant. Lenin said, "We'll treat the West as useful idiots who'll sell us the very rope that we'll use to hang them."

Now, I'm not here to say that Yeltsin's regime was a perfect democracy. I am very critical of Yeltsin, and I believe Russia missed great opportunities to become a proper democratic state with established institutions and a normal system of checks and balances. It didn't happen, and there is a lot of criticism levied at Yeltsin, which is justified. But again, we avoided wars; we avoided ethnic conflict. We could have had a war like in Yugoslavia, if someone like Putin had been in power then.

And yes, I agree, there was massive corruption under Boris Yeltsin, especially in his second term when the oligarchs were ripping off the country. These very people who were stealing money were the ones who convinced Yeltsin to appoint Putin to protect them. They didn't care about democracy; they wanted to protect themselves. And with very few exceptions, these people are still around.

When we talk about Putin's friends, we are talking about people who were lucky. They shared the same desk with Putin at school or were in judo class with him, and now they are on the *Forbes* wealthiest list. As Anne said, the country is owned by very few families, and ironically, they are all people who are close to Mr. Putin. They are fighting for power, and it's a fight for survival. The only item on Putin's agenda is to stay in power, and he will keep it by whatever means necessary because he has no other choice. He will commit any crime to ensure he can stay in the Kremlin.

RUDYARD GRIFFITHS: Ladies and gentlemen, both sides of the debate have spoken. Now we want to get into an exchange between debaters. Vladimir, let's start by asking you to pick up on something that Anne said. The Obama administration tried to roll back a number of policies that were seen as exclusionary to Russia. What did this famous reset do? It led to the conflict in Crimea and Ukraine. How do you respond to the perceived failure of that policy?

VLADIMIR POZNER: First of all, it did not. Secondly, Russia was so poor that they even misspelled the world "reset" in Russia. This policy did not lead to Crimea at all.

The bombardment of Yugoslavia is a perfect example of Russian humiliation; they begged us not to do it. And that was during Yeltsin's time. The Russians were told to just shut up. And since the UN would not condone it, NATO led the mission. And then, of course, Kosovo was allowed to leave Serbia, although it had been a part of Serbia for over five hundred years.

Why was that possible? Why were the Russians ignored? This is the kind of humiliation that has led to the greatest anti-American sentiment in Russia that I have ever known, much more than during Soviet times. The average Russian today is absolutely anti-American, which was not the case before. There was anti-Bush, anti-Reagan sentiment, yes, but not anti-Americanism. This feeling is rooted in truth; it's not just propaganda.

GARRY KASPAROV: No, there's a lot of propaganda. My mother is seventy-eight. She was born and raised under Stalin. She said she has never heard such a concentrated message of hatred 24/7 on Russian television, like there is now.

VLADIMIR POZNER: Why are you yelling?

ANNE APPLEBAUM: That's how he always talks.

GARRY KASPAROV: Because I am also Russian and I know Russia.

VLADIMIR POZNER: Oh, so Russians yell. That's the idea, right? They also drink vodka, dance, and play the balalaika.

GARRY KASPAROV: I don't drink.

VLADIMIR POZNER: Russians are normal people. Your mother has had her experience. I think I'm even older than your mother.

GARRY KASPAROV: Yes.

VLADIMIR POZNER: And I lived in the Soviet Union.

GARRY KASPAROV: But we lived on different sides of the fence. You were on the propaganda side; we were on the opposite side, listening to you.

VLADIMIR POZNER: No, that is not true. You don't know anything about me. The propaganda in Russia was very different back then. It was far less sophisticated because Russia was totally isolated.

GARRY KASPAROV: You mean during the Soviet Union? Today it is more sophisticated. I agree.

VLADIMIR POZNER: Yes, today it is much more sophisticated. It is much more dangerous. I'm certainly not saying it isn't, but the average Russian is also sadly more anti-American.

RUDYARD GRIFFITHS: Vladimir's saying that the policy of isolation is stoking the anti-American sentiments that empower Putin and his ruling clique. Anne, why don't you respond to that?

ANNE APPLEBAUM: We created Putin and his ruling clique. Our banking systems laundered their money and our tax havens protected it, so stop acting like they're somehow a reaction to our isolation. We kept Putin on board. We invited him to the meetings and we tried to make him part of things. Initially, it was with very good intentions.

We wanted Putin to be part of the West. We had this idea that Russia was a candidate Western country and if we were just nice enough, they would join us. What we've discovered is that it has evolved into something really quite different. It's not the Soviet Union. Soviet analogies are wrong. But it's not Nazi Germany, either. It's a very new, very sophisticated kind of propaganda-run state.

This is a country in which every single television channel and every single newspaper and almost every single Internet web site, with a few exceptions, is controlled by the state and run in such a way that they all appear to be slightly different. This is not one *Pravda* saying one thing every day. This is a wide spectrum of different media that all say the same thing using different perspectives and tones: the tabloid way, the sophisticated way, the entertaining way, or the news-focused way.

They're telling people the same stories that Putin wants them to hear. And the story they've been telling for many months now is bitterly anti-American, bitterly anti-European, and coming very close to being warmongering in a way that I don't remember.

The hatred toward Ukraine; the hatred toward Americans; the use of semi-fascist symbolism — this is something really, really new and different. No wonder people are anti-American.

RUDYARD GRIFFITHS: So is engagement nearly impossible because there isn't a partner on the other side?

STEPHEN F. COHEN: Well, I'm having a hard time, because I tried to sign a contract with the audience whereby we would deal with some facts. I read ten Russian newspapers a day, and —

ANNE APPLEBAUM: How many Ukrainian newspapers do you read?

STEPHEN F. COHEN: I read ten Russian newspapers a day, across the spectrum. What Ms. Applebaum is describing is true in at least three of those ten — you hear the same story. But this is not the case in the other seven. There are at least three newspapers that are very pro-European, pro-American, and very critical of Putin.

What is astonishing for me to learn is that oligarchs and states launder money offshore. I had no idea such things happened in the world. I see a bigger problem in Russia because of the way this economic system formed in the 1990s. It absolutely has to be reformed.

Do I think it is Ms. Applebaum's right to tell Russia or force Russia to do it? Absolutely not, because the result will be worse. This is for Russians to decide — not us. We need to decide if we need a Russian security partner in Russia, whether it is Putin or his successor.

And I would end with this point: I do not ever recall — and I've been around a long time — hearing people whom Ms. Applebaum and Mr. Kasparov represent speaking about a Soviet Communist leader in this way. In fact, when I listen to them, I have to say that there seems to be kind of a repressed nostalgia for the Soviet Union in their vendetta against Putin's Russia.

ANNE APPLEBAUM: When you were giving your first introduction, Mr. Cohen, I wrote down "repressed Soviet nostalgia" on my notepad. You spoke with nostalgia of the days when the Soviet Union was still around and could help us regulate the world. This is what you dream of.

The Cold War era is something for which I have no nostalgia — half of Europe was enslaved during that period. Totalitarianism ruled hundreds of millions of people. You have this idea that if only the U.S. and Russia could work together once again we could create some kind of stability. Russia is not a country that wants stability. Russia is interested in chaos. It created chaos in Ukraine.

RUDYARD GRIFFITHS: Garry, let me bring you in here. Some would suggest that the recent Russia-Iran deal helped defuse that conflict. And some would say that Russia saved Obama's proverbial bacon on his squiggly red line in Syria over chemical weapons. How do you respond to those examples of Russian co-operation?

GARRY KASPAROV: Co-operation implies that you make concessions and that you do something that may hurt you and your interests in order to bolster your relationship with your partner. In both cases, Russian interests are winning. Russia has been supplying Iran with nuclear technology, so let's not forget that this uranium goes to Russia. Russia will hold the key, which enhances Putin's position in the international arena.

And let's not forget that these negotiations went on forever, and Putin's interest was always to keep the pressure on in the region because it helped to push up oil prices, something vital to Putin's financial survival.

As for Syria, Putin's priority from day one was to save a mass murderer named Bashar al-Assad, and he's succeeded. There are many reasons why he stepped in to do so: one was probably some form of dictators' brotherhood. Believe me, after so many dictators were washed away by public anger in the Arab world, Putin didn't want to allow Assad to be toppled because then Russians could see that dictators were also vulnerable.

And let's not forget that Putin is always looking at the map of the pipelines. Gas supplies are very important. They are his grip on Europe. Syria is potentially vital for a Qatar, Iraq, Syria, and Turkey pipeline, which could make Russian gas redundant. So in both cases Putin played the role of a saviour — the white knight at the eleventh hour — but he was the greatest beneficiary.

RUDYARD GRIFFITHS: How do you all respond to that?

VLADIMIR POZNER: If Mr. Kasparov is saying that Putin stands up for Russia's interests, then I would have to suppose that he does, from a certain viewpoint. I read your interview opposite mine in the newspaper where you kind of laugh at Putin's popularity. You know as well as I do that the people who did the poll — the Levada-Centre — are honest people.

The poll was not government sponsored — the Levada-Centre is a very respectable organization. The poll showed that over 80 percent of Russian people support Putin. Now, there has got to be some reason for it. These are not stupid people. Propaganda is propaganda, but these are people who have lived in the country a long time. They know what propaganda is. So what do they see in Putin?

I'm not defending Putin; I'm explaining a situation. What they see in Putin is a man who has brought Russia back. Russians no longer feel that they are in second place, that they are not a great nation. They've been told by others previously to just get out of our face. And now they can say, we're back and if you don't like us we don't care. But we're back thanks to Putin. This is the sentiment and something that has to be understood, whether good or bad. It is a fact. And there is a reason for it. It's not just because Russia is an autocratic state. When my colleague, Stephen F. Cohen, talks about the Russian media he is right. There is a lot of media that would dispute what Ms. Applebaum is describing, like *Novaya Gazeta*, *Komsomolskaya Pravda*, and *Moskovskij Komsomolets*.

ANNE APPLEBAUM: We give you *Novaya Gazeta*.

VLADIMIR POZNER: What I'm saying is that they are about as different as ABC, NBC, and CBS. It's propaganda on both sides.

GARRY KASPAROV: Wow.

ANNE APPLEBAUM: I haven't heard that kind of moral equivalence in a long time.

VLADIMIR POZNER: The people here do not read Ukrainian or Russian newspapers, so they don't know what's happening.

GARRY KASPAROV: When was the last time you were in Kiev?

VLADIMIR POZNER: This is funny. I was in Kiev two and some years ago to receive the honourary title of Man of the Year of Ukraine.

RUDYARD GRIFFITHS: There we go: Man of the Year of Ukraine. Let me bring Stephen into this conversation.

STEPHEN F. COHEN: I hope you noticed that the chess master just got checkmated. Look, I understand this fixation on Putin. I really do. Personally, I don't care much about Putin. I wish I were going to live long enough to see how my fellow historians evaluate Putin's role as a leader of Russia. And I think it is going to be a big debate, the positives and the negatives.

But let me address the elephant in the room: Wasn't NATO expanding toward Russia's borders when we were supposedly embracing the country in the 1990s?

Think about it like this: What if I found out where you lived and parked all my military equipment across the street. And then I told you that I was just there for your security. I'm making sure no one breaks into your house. And then I notice that you've brought a few folks around who have brought all their military equipment, and that now you're across the street from my house, too. But don't worry because its all for your security — NATO is about democracy and you need democracy.

Let's be serious. We were continuously warned by liberal Russians — people we liked in Russia — that we were pushing too far. Eventually, rightly or wrongly, the Russian political elite decided that this expansion of NATO was a way of making sure Russia would forever be a subservient state to the West.

And the brass ring — or rather, the silver ring — in all of this was Georgia. A proxy war ensued in 2008 as a result. Ukraine has also been another brass ring; it is openly spoken about in Washington.

If you think this is good policy, and if you believe we

should push our power as close to Russia as we can and bring Ukraine into the Western security system because it's ultimately good for us, then say so and then let's debate that issue. But don't go on about the demon Putin, because the Russian understanding of Ukraine mirrors the concept of NATO expansion from the beginning.

The Russians invaded Ukraine because the Russian political class believed that NATO was on its way not only to Kiev, but also to Crimea. Now, we can say that's crazy, but perception in politics is everything. If you isolate Russia, they're going to perceive it in an even more extreme form, and we will never be safe.

RUDYARD GRIFFITHS: Let's hear from Anne on NATO.

ANNE APPLEBAUM: I'll say this because you invited me to, Mr. Cohen, but that's crazy. First of all, why did NATO expand? Let's tick back the clock again to the 1990s. Who wanted expansion? It was the central Europeans who wanted it. It was not an American idea. I remember because I was in Warsaw at the time. The central Europeans wanted it because they were afraid: they were afraid of Russia, even then. They saw what Russia was becoming.

The United States very reluctantly agreed to expand the security zone so that the people — all 100 million of them — would be able to transition to democracy and begin economic development and growth without fear of invasion. And it worked. It was unbelievably successful.

STEPHEN F. COHEN: It worked?

ANNE APPLEBAUM: It worked for the central Europeans: a hundred million people were safe. A region that had been the source of two world wars has not been a source of conflict since then. How did we do it? The strategy was carried out in a manner designed to reassure Russia from the beginning. Russia was included in every piece of negotiation. No NATO bases were ever placed in the new member states.

Until 2013, no exercises were ever conducted in new member states. In response to Russian objections — and this is a very important point — both Ukraine and Georgia were openly and definitively denied NATO membership in 2008, which has been repeated ever since. It is no longer on the table. Mr. Cohen, why are you looking at me that way?

STEPHEN F. COHEN: In 2008?

ANNE APPLEBAUM: In 2008 at a NATO meeting, they said there would be no membership plan for Ukraine and Georgia. And since then it hasn't been on the table.

STEPHEN F. COHEN: They said something else at that meeting in 2008, that NATO membership remains open to Georgia and Ukraine.

ANNE APPLEBAUM: Yes, theoretically, which means it remains open to Russia as well.

STEPHEN F. COHEN: Oh, please.

RUDYARD GRIFFITHS: Vladimir, let's hear from you on this topic. I know it's something you feel strongly about.

ANNE APPLEBAUM: No, wait. I haven't finished my point yet. Since 2008, Russia has been rebuilding its military, invading one neighbour after another, while the American army scaled back its European forces, so much so that by 2013 there was not one single American tank in Europe. You think this is an aggressive policy? There is no way that Putin believed that NATO was a genuine military threat. This is propaganda he has been using at home as a way to consolidate his power.

VLADIMIR POZNER: The us-versus-NATO discussion in no way consolidates his power at home. As far as the Russian people are concerned the issue has nothing to do with his power. But NATO has everything to do with the Russian psyche. And perception, as has been said, is very important. Let me remind you of what happened in 1962.

In 1962, two independent countries — the Soviet Union and Cuba — agreed to put Soviet missiles on Cuban soil, the reason being that there were American missiles in Turkey and the Soviets decided it would be a good idea to have their missiles closer to the United States. This was in the height of the Cold War. Two countries have the right to make that kind of decision, but when the United States found out that this was happening, it said, Not in our backyard. The U.S. demanded that the missiles be removed and said, We will sink your ships if we have to. We were on the verge of World War III and all parties seemed okay with that fate. These are facts.

ANNE APPLEBAUM: Mr. Pozner, one of the things negotiated with—

VLADIMIR POZNER: May I finish my—

ANNE APPLEBAUM: No, you can't.

VLADIMIR POZNER: Well, thank you very much for exhibiting the way the West speaks to Russia.

ANNE APPLEBAUM: One of the things negotiated with Russia was an agreement not to move nuclear missiles. That is a fact that you left out.

VLADIMIR POZNER: I disagree with you—that agreement did not happen. Rightly or wrongly, this is the way Russia looks at NATO. It sees it as a threat. NATO was created to protect the West from a possible Soviet invasion, but there is no more Soviet Union and there has not been one for over twenty-five years. The Warsaw Pact, which was the Soviet's answer to NATO, is no longer upheld.

I tend to trust Mikhail Gorbachev. He told me three times that James Baker, the then U.S. secretary of state, expressed to him that if they agreed to the unification of Germany and took down the Berlin Wall, NATO would not move one inch to the east. Now, you may say he's lying, but I think he's telling the truth. During the Soviet period, which didn't last very long after that, NATO did not move to the east. It only shifted under Clinton.

And when the Russians questioned this move east under Clinton, Yeltsin was told that they didn't have an agreement. The U.S. said, We had an agreement with the Soviet Union, but you're Russia. And so in 1991, Poland and Czechoslovakia, which was still Czechoslovakia back then, became members of NATO. And finally, NATO found itself on Russia's border, in Estonia and Latvia.

You may think that there's nothing dangerous about the whole scenario. I'm telling you — and this is perhaps a holdover of the Cold War mentality — that NATO is seen as a threat. In regards to Ukraine, the Russians have said, We will not allow NATO to be on our border in the southwest; we will not allow it, just as America did not allow the missiles in Cuba. You can condone it, or not condone it, but that is how it is perceived.

RUDYARD GRIFFITHS: Garry?

GARRY KASPAROV: A couple of points. One is about Russian leaders, the elites. Mr. Cohen repeatedly said there are no Russian elites making decisions. In fact, there is one man who makes all the decisions. And by the way, these Russian elites, as a combined entity, know exactly where to put their kids, their money, their fortunes: south Kensington in London, Miami, probably in this country as well. So this whole idea of the Russian elites being afraid of the West is not true because they know that they can be safe with their fortunes and their future generations here.

Another myth, which I have heard repeatedly tonight, is that Putin is very popular. I don't want to argue with you about the Levada-Centre's integrity. I give them full credit. But what is an opinion poll? Somebody calls you anonymously and asks what you think about Mr. Putin. You know, it makes me really proud of my country that 20 percent of people said they didn't like Putin, knowing it could be the KGB on the other end of the phone.

We're being accused of being Cold Warriors, war-mongering crazies, but we want to live in the twenty-first century. We are hearing about the nineteenth and twentieth centuries, in America and Russia. Sometimes I hear about Germany. What about the countries in between? I believe those people have the same rights.

VLADIMIR POZNER: I agree.

GARRY KASPAROV: I was in Kiev two weeks ago, not two years ago. And I was proud to meet this young Ukrainian who stood against the corrupt regime of Viktor Yanukovych. I believe it is the right of Ukrainians to decide what will happen to their country. Support for NATO membership in Ukraine eighteen months ago was merely 16 or 17 percent. It's now quadrupled. Guess why?

It is not always Russians and Ukrainians at war there, against each other. I spoke to many people who fought on the eastern front against Russia, and most of them are ethnic Russians. They are fighting Putin's invading armies because they don't want to live in Putin's Russia. This is the Russia I want to see.

VLADIMIR POZNER: Good.

RUDYARD GRIFFITHS: Okay, Stephen and then Anne.

STEPHEN F. COHEN: But we're back to Putin again. Are we going to have a discussion of what is in the best interest of the West? That really is embedded in the question, isn't it? Should we engage Russia or should we have a debate about how we are going to get rid of Putin?

Ms. Applebaum wrote a wonderful book of history called *Gulag*, and I strongly recommend you read it if you have an interest in the subject because a master historian is at work there. But now comes the "however."

I understand that, for one reason or another, she views this whole saga of NATO expansion from the perspective of central and eastern Europe. But the story she told of NATO expansion is written nowhere in the history books we have now. There was tremendous pressure on Clinton in the United States to go back on the word that had been given to Gorbachev about NATO expansion. The whole history of NATO expansion that we've heard tonight is the fairy-tale version: NATO expanded to protect and save central and eastern European countries from a menacing Russia while bringing democracy along the way. But it isn't the true story.

There is another debate we should be having here, though some of you won't even like the question: Does a nation, any nation, have the right to join NATO if it technically qualifies for membership? I don't think it does.

NATO is a security organization. It's not the Chamber of Commerce. It's not a non-selective sorority or fraternity. You get in if we like you. It's a security organization and the only criterion that matters is, does this country's membership enhance our security?

NATO has brought us the greatest crisis in international affairs since the Cuban Missile Crisis. And a lot of people, including NATO member states, are rethinking the organization. Read what the Czech president has been saying, or what is being said in Hungary or in the other half of Poland. There are a lot of fundamental questions about whether or not this has really enhanced the security of Europe. But that is the subject for another debate. You don't get a debate with opinion; you get one with facts. And these are facts.

GARRY KASPAROV: The president of the Czech Republic, Miloš Zeman, received campaign funds from Lukoil, the Russian oil company. And he was defied by his own parliament.

ANNE APPLEBAUM: Yes.

RUDYARD GRIFFITHS: I want to be conscious of time, but I'd like to deal with a topic that is on a lot of people's minds. Anne, you and I spoke about this earlier so I want you to answer it for the audience. It's about the presence of nuclear weapons, the large nuclear arsenal that Russia has at its disposal. I'm sure many people would naturally feel a tendency to come over to the compromise camp on the basis that we just can't afford to get this wrong. We can't risk the potential for an escalation that could flow from a policy of isolation. How do you respond to that?

ANNE APPLEBAUM: First I want to respond to Mr. Pozner, who didn't let me correct him. One of the other elements of NATO expansion, which was very important, was an agreement to not move nuclear missiles, an agreement which the West has kept. This is why the Cuban Missile Crisis analogy is completely wrong.

VLADIMIR POZNER: It's not wrong at all. It's fear.

ANNE APPLEBAUM: Fear has nothing to do with it.

VLADIMIR POZNER: It's fear on both sides.

ANNE APPLEBAUM: Okay, so there is fear. But what is the answer to the question about nuclear missiles? Fear and fear of nuclear weapons is very central to this issue. It actually explains why we aren't more enthusiastic about helping Ukraine. If Ukraine were being invaded by Belarus, we might give them some radar weapons and not worry about it. Why don't we help Ukraine? It is because we're afraid of Russia's nuclear arsenal. And we are also afraid, as one of my opponents said, that this is an irrational country that might sell nuclear weapons to other people one of these days. We don't know what it might do. It might run off the ranch and do something crazy. How have we dealt with a country like that in the past? It is called deterrence. Deterrence is not an aggressive policy. It is not an offensive policy. It is defensive.

The deterrence argument is premised on the idea that if you bomb us, we will bomb you back. It is a very unattractive policy and no one likes it. It's MAD or Dr. Strangelove; it's a horrible thought, but this is the only policy we have right now that works. It is the only policy that we are capable of using now toward Putin's Russia, which does not want to engage with us anymore. Russia today pumps out propaganda against us in all kinds of different ways in all kinds of countries, whether it's, as Garry says, funding the Czech president's election or funding the far right in France. This is a country that does not want to be part of our system anymore and has made that very clear.

What can we do? We can deter. We need to ensure that our awareness of Putin's dictatorial practices goes all the way up to the Kremlin. And the word "cronies" is an important one. Because what are they? They are just a bunch of rich guys who are friends of his but are somehow very powerful. What other word do we have to describe them? We need to ensure that Putin's cronies know we will respond if provoked. We don't have a better policy.

I watched all of this happen; I've read the history of the Soviet Union; I've watched the transition and now we're back to exactly the place I would have never wanted us to be. In some ways it is one of the great tragedies of my life.

VLADIMIR POZNER: I think we're in a much worse place than we were, quite frankly, because back then there were two ideologies facing each other. Now there is no ideology in Russia.

ANNE APPLEBAUM: Oh, yes there is.

VLADIMIR POZNER: No, for most people there isn't. They don't even know what the future holds, or what they are working for. Whether or not this was true back in the Soviet days is a different issue.

ANNE APPLEBAUM: The good old days!

VLADIMIR POZNER: No, those were terrible days, but it was an ideology from the beginning. You know as well as I do that the Red Scare was about ideology. It is no longer about ideology now. It is geopolitical. It is about whose interests are at stake.

RUDYARD GRIFFITHS: So why does this put us in a more dangerous position?

VLADIMIR POZNER: Because it is unpredictable. And something else has changed: back in the bad old days, there was real fear of nuclear weapons. Children hid under desks, and movies came out like *The Day After*. People were very aware. Today, people don't even talk about nuclear weapons.

ANNE APPLEBAUM: Except in Poland.

VLADIMIR POZNER: It's very dangerous. They're not talking about them anywhere.

ANNE APPLEBAUM: That is not correct.

VLADIMIR POZNER: They're not present in our conversations the way they used to be. And I think that's a bad thing.

RUDYARD GRIFFITHS: I'm going to go to Garry to comment on this point and then I'm going to give Vladimir and Stephen the last word.

GARRY KASPAROV: I wish nobody ever had to talk about nuclear weapons. But Russian television has been talking about them over and over again for the last year, and threatening the West. What about those big billboards that promote turning America into radioactive ash?

VLADIMIR POZNER: You have one person saying that, come on.

GARRY KASPAROV: That's Channel Two, Russian television: one person says it but 100 million people are watching and listening. Putin publicly says he would use nukes if the West stood up to him in Crimea.

VLADIMIR POZNER: He did not say he would use nukes.

GARRY KASPAROV: He did.

STEPHEN F. COHEN: They talked about going on high alert, but the United States has been on high alert a dozen times.

VLADIMIR POZNER: Let's be a little bit more precise. He did not say he would use nukes. Khrushchev said, "We will bury you" back in the 1950s. Remember that?

GARRY KASPAROV: Yes. I read that in the books, and I've listened to Putin.

VLADIMIR POZNER: Do you even know the idiot who said that we'll turn you into radioactive ash? His name is Dmitry Kiselyov and I saw him say it on television, so it wasn't Putin. It's as if you listened to Rush Limbaugh and he said something along those lines and you inferred that he represented the viewpoint of all Americans. If you'll excuse me, this Dmitry guy is a jerk for saying such things.

GARRY KASPAROV: You are free to have jerks of all stripes on American television, but not in Russia. In Russia you are only allowed one.

VLADIMIR POZNER: But it's not a Russian policy. It's one person. And that's very clear.

RUDYARD GRIFFITHS: Let's get Stephen in here.

GARRY KASPAROV: Limbaugh is not on the White House payroll. The person who said that was on the Kremlin payroll. That is the difference.

RUDYARD GRIFFITHS: Stephen, let's give you the final say on this topic: How does the threat of nuclear weapons flow into the discussion of isolation versus engagement?

STEPHEN F. COHEN: I will take the rabbinical view here that both Kasparov and Pozner are right. Talk of nuclear weapons has re-emerged, but not in the same way that we were conscious of during the Cold War. Ms. Applebaum wrote a column recently that essentially said we should rattle our nuclear weapons, which concerned me.

It is absurd for people to be talking like that, and Ms. Applebaum has already echoed her column's sentiments here today. We are wading into dangerous territory. I would ring the alarm even more than Mr. Pozner and suggest that we are living in a new Cold War and it is potentially more dangerous than the last one. This is where the nuclear weapons come in, for several reasons.

First, the epicentre of the last Cold War was in Berlin. This one is in Ukraine, right on Russia's border, so imagine the possibilities for provocation, mistakes, and all the rest.

Second is something that really worries me: during the last Cold War, over forty years ago, the great powers developed a series of rules of conduct—hot phones, hot-lines, constant discussion, meetings—that kept us safe. There are no rules of conduct yet in this new Cold War. And that is why anything can happen.

A third reason is that there is no opposition to another Cold War in the United States, and there was a lot of opposition to it before. You will remember that one of the great achievements of Reagan and Gorbachev was to eliminate intermediate-range cruise missiles — and this is the only time a category of nuclear weapons has been eliminated, ever. That was 1987, if I'm not mistaken. It was an enormous achievement that made everybody safer. These missiles need only four or five minutes to reach their targets.

Now both sides are talking about reintroducing intermediate-range cruise missiles. The Russians are talking about putting them in Crimea and Kaliningrad. The United States is talking about putting them back in western Europe. This is extremely dangerous.

RUDYARD GRIFFITHS: We're going to move to closing statements. Let's have Garry Kasparov up first. Garry, you've got three minutes.

GARRY KASPAROV: I will have to ask for Mr. Cohen's forgiveness, because I want to talk about Vladimir Putin again. There are differences between the Soviet Union and Russia today, because, as Mr. Pozner said, in the bad old days there was the politburo. The ten worst people in the world can make more balanced decisions than one man. And with Vladimir Putin there is no way out. He presents himself as a strongman who can protect Russia against endless enemies.

And I've said from the very beginning of this debate, since I am a Russian patriot, that I want to see my country free and strong and able to play a role — a positive role — in the world. I don't want to hear the same jokes as the ones that recently have been revived in eastern Europe. For example, Putin is entering the country and is asked by a customs officer, "Occupation?" And he answers, "Yes, of course."

This is not the image of Russia I want to see projected. It is hard for me to argue for isolation, but this is not the isolation of Russia — this is the isolation of a dictator. The strength of a dictator is like the strength of a mafia boss, the *capo di tutti capi*, the ringleader of all. He maintains power not because he is elected or because he has a birthright but because he protects everybody and is invincible, so nobody can go after him. And he prevails as long as he keeps this image of the strongman. And every time the free world makes concessions to him, he becomes more and more arrogant.

If Putin is not stopped in Ukraine, he will continue to move further outside of Russia. He will start provocations in the Baltic countries in order to undermine NATO because he needs chaos and muddy waters. That is the way for him to survive politically. It is all about domestic politics, because he has nothing else to offer besides foreign policy expansion.

On the subject of isolation again, we spoke a lot about the Cold War, and Henry Kissinger was mentioned. I was a kid, but I remember him and learned more about him later on. In 1974 there was a big debate in the U.S. Senate about the Jackson-Vanik Amendment. It was a provision that proposed tying trade with human rights in the Soviet Union.

Mr. Kissinger spoke against it. There was a great man, Andrei Sakharov, my role model, who was harassed and eventually ended up in exile. He promoted what you may call isolation, in order to weaken the regime.

It is very important that we send this message not just to Putin but also to his cronies. His cronies, or inner circle, the Russian bureaucracy, and the middle class in Moscow, all need to understand that the policies of engagement that enhance Russia's strength will no longer continue. And the free world will stand behind its values and will not think about Putin's Russia but about the future of my great country. Thank you.

RUDYARD GRIFFITHS: Three minutes, Stephen.

STEPHEN F. COHEN: I was going to begin with a light-hearted remark and say that it would really be fun just to see Kasparov and Pozner go after each other one-on-one. I was in Moscow in early March in kitchens where Russians on both sides of the political spectrum had exactly these types of conversations. So a big debate goes on in Russia.

But when Kasparov said that he thought Sakharov was going to be on his side today, I suddenly felt, I wouldn't say angry, but I would say really disappointed. Some things should be sacred, and I think Sakharov's name is one of them. Under absolutely no circumstances would Sakharov have supported Russian isolation. Everything the father of the Soviet hydrogen bomb wrote promoted engagement on these issues. You need to go back and read. Worshipping somebody without reading them is probably not the right way to go.

The same thing can be said about Putin. I am not

pro-Putin. I have no sentimental attachment to Putin whatsoever. As a historian, he's a subject of study to me. Start reading what Putin actually says, including the speech he gave when he annexed Crimea. He said, "They have driven us into a corner and we have nowhere to retreat to." He's talking about NATO. He's talking about the encroachment on Ukraine.

Isolation will only exacerbate those distorted perceptions of us, assuming you think they're distorted. So let me end by returning to an astonishing thing that Ms. Applebaum said. She said that Putin's Russia does not want to be part of our system any longer, which implies the old Russia wanted to be, but Russia under Putin no longer wants to be. It's a strange statement because, first of all, you can go to the Kremlin web site in English and read every dangerous speech Putin has given: he is on his knees pleading to be part of the West and lamenting that he has been driven out of it.

Don't put your hands up, Garry. I would not come here and lie to you. Read his last six or seven large speeches on the Ukrainian crisis.

There is one other thing: Russia was never part of our system. I said at the beginning of this debate that I would focus on facts, not opinions. Ms. Applebaum omitted an important detail with her fairy-tale story about NATO expansion. The fact is, NATO expansion excluded Russia from the post-Soviet European system of security. How can they not want to be part of a system of which they were never made a part?

RUDYARD GRIFFITHS: Anne.

ANNE APPLEBAUM: Ladies and gentlemen, it has no doubt been a very confusing evening. You have just heard two very radically different accounts of contemporary Russia. You have heard on one side that Russia is a little bit difficult, but that it is the kind of state we need to speak to and engage with. Our opponents argue that we need to talk to Russia, and that it is very important that we are reasonable so that we can continue to divide up the world the way we once did twenty-five years ago. I don't really want to support this approach because I'm not really pro-Putin.

On our side, you've heard an argument that Russia is actually a nation that thinks differently. The reason we keep talking about Putin and his cronies is because he is an owner-occupier — these are owner-occupiers. They are not just politicians. They own Gazprom. The owners of Gazprom are the leaders of the country. They use their businesses and their media inside their country, inside Ukraine, inside central Europe, and all over the West in order to achieve their own ends.

And what are their ends? They want to remain in power. Everything that Putin does is to support his ultimate goal of maintaining power, whether it's building up his nuclear arsenal, carrying out military exercises, claiming that Malaysian planes were shot down by Martians, or whatever else it may be. We are forced to talk about him because he is so dominant.

Our side of the debate, and certainly not our opponents, have not talked enough about the people who have been the most important victims of the West's policy of engagement until now: the young, energized Ukrainians who stood on the Maidan last year in the cold in order to fight Putin-style corruption and dictatorship. In the past eighteen months, these men and women have created new television stations from scratch; run for parliament and won on anti-corruption tickets; and have set up organizations designed to promote good government and transparency.

They may well not succeed, since they have extraordinary obstacles to overcome, but their goal is to create a more democratic, fair, and less corrupt world in the twenty-first century, and Putin's Russia is trying to stop them. I repeat: Ukraine is not Putin's only target. He also wants to undermine our societies, corrupt our politicians, and spread conspiracies inside our media. He hopes to persuade Europeans to succumb to the old temptations of the fascist far right.

To stop this from happening, and to stop him from destroying Ukraine, we need to isolate Russia by enforcing our own corruption laws, disentangling ourselves from the drug of Russian money, and re-establishing Western solidarity, which he is trying to destroy.

RUDYARD GRIFFITHS: Mr. Pozner, you have the last word.

VLADIMIR POZNER: Thank you. I refuse to play this game of who's nice and who's not. I care about Russia so I'm only going to ask you one question: What are the consequences of isolating Russia? Well, on my count, there is a minimum of ten. And all ten are detrimental to the West.

First, it plays into the hands of the chauvinist, anti-Western forces in Russia that dream of bringing down the Iron Curtain again. Second, it plays into the hands of the traditionally anti-Western Russian Orthodox Church. Third, it reinforces the feeling now shared by 73 percent of all Russians that the West, led by the United States, is the enemy. Fourth, it turns Russia eastward into a partnership with communist China, a partnership that is both dangerous and threatening to the West. Fifth, it makes Russia ever more unpredictable. Sixth, it plays into the hands of Russia's military industrial complex. Seventh, it reinforces the traditional Russian desire to circle the wagons in view of what seems like a hostile environment. Eighth, it minimizes any outside information for the Russian people who presently have access to Western media, movies, and to the Internet. Ninth, it cuts off travel for all average citizens, including for tourism, exchanges, and educational opportunities. And tenth, it leads to the birth of a generation of Russians hostile to the West.

What are the consequences of the West engaging Russia? By engaging Russia, I mean opening its doors to as many Russians as is physically possible, easing visa restrictions or waiving them altogether, allowing Russians to visit, to work, to send their children to schools and universities, to develop human contacts. By doing so, the West will achieve a profound change in people's mindsets, which will fundamentally change the country's politics and its policies. It will not happen overnight. But it will inevitably happen. And this beyond a shadow of a doubt will be a huge benefit for the West and, by the same token, for Russia and for the Russian people.

And, finally, I'd like to say that if, as Ms. Applebaum once wrote, the Russian president dreams of setting down a new Iron Curtain, well then isolating Russia is playing right into Mr. Putin's hands. Thank you very much.

RUDYARD GRIFFITHS: Ladies and gentlemen, we've been treated to a superb hour and a half tonight. I want to thank our debaters; on behalf of the entire audience, bravo! And again, thank you to the Aurea Foundation for making this all possible. This is the kind of informed conversation that benefits us all, regardless of what side of this issue you stand on.

Summary: The pre-debate vote was 58 percent in favour of the resolution and 42 percent against it. The final vote showed 48 percent in favour of the motion and 52 against. Given that more of the voters shifted to the team against the resolution, the victory goes to Anne Applebaum and Garry Kasparov.

Pre-Debate Interviews

ANNE APPLEBAUM IN CONVERSATION
WITH RUDYARD GRIFFITHS

RUDYARD GRIFFITHS: A great pleasure to have Anne Applebaum with me. She will be arguing against tonight's motion, "Be it resolved the West should engage not isolate Russia." She is a Pulitzer Prize–winning author, columnist for the *Washington Post*, and someone who has thought long and hard about eastern Europe, Soviet Russia, and now post-Soviet Russia. Anne, you have come all the way from Warsaw to be a part of this debate, and we really appreciate that. What is the mood in periphery countries such as Poland at the moment, looking at the events that are unfolding in Ukraine?

ANNE APPLEBAUM: They are frightened. There is a bit of a "we told you so" mood. This is what we have been afraid of for a long time. Some of them have been talking about it—worrying about it—for many years. Even though some of these countries are in NATO, and part of the Western alliance, there is still fear because people are wondering if the Western alliance still exists. Is it still strong enough to protect us? People are nervous about invasion. They are also nervous that their political system is being undermined in other ways. Russians are famous for using disinformation and support for radical political parties to undermine democracies. And they are afraid this could happen to them or in what we used to call western Europe, which could weaken them.

RUDYARD GRIFFITHS: From your perspective, I know isolating Russia is the answer. But what does that look like? More specifically, do you think the current sanctions against Russia are sufficient in the aftermath of Crimea and Ukraine, or do you have a broader, more expansive, idea for isolation?

ANNE APPLEBAUM: Let's be clear that "isolation" is your word and is not the word that I would ever have used to discuss this topic. It's an awkward word to have to defend in this context. And I'm sorry that I have to do it, because of course I am somebody who has been arguing for engagement and for the integration of eastern Europe with western Europe for twenty-five years. I initially hoped that we would have engaged Russia too. I was a part of a lot of different groups and initiatives that were designed to do just that at school. We promoted civic education and democracy in Russia and I have been in favour of that my whole adult life.

Unfortunately, we are now at a stage where the nature of this particular Russian regime has become so dangerous and so toxic, not only to its own citizens, which is a whole separate subject, but also to its immediate neighbours, and to all of Europe, and to the Western alliance, that engagement is not possible. I think we really need to think in terms of getting Russian influence out of our societies. This is just a first step, but it means getting corrupt Russian money out of our financial systems and getting rid of money that Russia pays to Western politicians. Russia buys politicians all over Europe: they bought Gerhard Schröder, who is a former German chancellor who now works for Gazprom. They pay influencers and former politicians, and even current political leaders in order to support their line.

We need to be much more conscious of this type of behaviour and get it out of our system. We need to make sure that influence is not part of our political debates. The Russian attempt to flirt with and enhance the power of the far right parties in Europe is part of what I'm talking about. So we need to disengage with Russia to make sure it's not influencing us.

And finally, we need to ensure that Russia's influence on Ukraine and its influence on eastern Europe is understood not only as political influence but also as a kind of disinformation. We need to understand that Russia uses false information and phony stories in order to create false images of what is happening. We need to also disengage from Russian media. We need to make sure that we understand there is a difference between true and false, because it is becoming harder and harder to distinguish.

One of the really strange and surprising things about the Ukraine debate over the last year and a half is how effective Russian propaganda has been and how Russian lies appear even in the West. Sometimes they create fake web sites, which sell fake stories that manage to get into the mainstream media. Sometimes it's more direct, and sometimes it's just Russia Today or many of the other Russian disinformation channels.

But it is really effective, and we need to understand how weak our media is, particularly in the era of budget cuts. We need to start thinking about how to keep that kind of negative influence out of our media space so at least we know what's going on in the world and we are not affected by this kind of systematic lying that the Russian regime produces.

RUDYARD GRIFFITHS: Your opponents are probably going to say tonight that by taking a stance of isolation versus engagement or by pushing back against Russia as opposed to reaching out, you're empowering very hard-liners around Putin and maybe even Putin himself. Putin and his cronies want Russia isolated to the degree that it enhances their own control over that society. How do you respond to that line of thinking?

ANNE APPLEBAUM: We have created Putin. Our policy of engagement for the last ten years — as well-intentioned as it was — created Putin. Allowing Russian companies access to our financial markets and our tax havens and our money laundering schemes have created the Russian oligarchy. The Russian oligarchy wouldn't exist if it wasn't for the Western banking system that supports it. We helped create Putin. We gave Russia its post-Soviet status. We gave Russia a seat at the UN. We invited Russia to join the G8. We allowed Putin to grow even when it was already clear which way his regime was going from the mid-2000s.

We let him hold an enormous G8 summit in St. Petersburg, where he was lionized and surrounded by all the leaders of the democratic world. He was able to use the summit to say to his people, Look, you say I'm not a democrat, but all these democratic countries here think I am. And in that way, we supported him. We allowed him to do what he's done.

The other problem is that the West is so nervous about Russia. I once went and looked up the obituaries that were written about Russian leaders after they had died, or, in the case of Khrushchev, when he resigned. At the time of Stalin's death in 1953, the *Times* of London wrote a long article, and the thrust of it was, now that Stalin is gone, the hard-liners in the wings will take over. Who is more of a hard-liner than Stalin? Stalin was a mass murderer. But we wrote the same thing when Brezhnev died and when Khrushchev resigned.

We have always been afraid that it will always get worse. Whatever we are doing, we really have to be careful of enhancing the hard-liners. But who knows, maybe Putin is the worst and maybe we'll get somebody better next.

RUDYARD GRIFFITHS: Some people tonight will probably be thinking about Putin's nuclear arsenal of 3,000-plus warheads and how that fundamentally changes the conversation, in the sense that accommodation and engagement really is the only course of action in the face of the potentially existential threat that the arsenal represents. Do you agree?

ANNE APPLEBAUM: There is a different response. I agree with you that this is all about nuclear weapons. I mean, we could help Ukraine if it had been invaded by Belarus. It wouldn't be that difficult. They would only need a couple of radars or something and some anti-tank weapons. The reason we don't help is because we are afraid of Putin's nuclear weapons. The reason diplomacy unfolds the way that it does in Europe is because we are afraid of Putin's nuclear weapons.

But the lessons of history show us that the way to cope with a country that has nuclear weapons is to deter it, and deterrence is not the same thing as engagement. Deterrence means building up your own credibility, building up your own forces, and making sure that the other person with nuclear weapons understands that if he uses them so will you. It's an unpleasant truth and it is one that I wish didn't exist. I am one of those people who would happily wish away nuclear weapons. But if somebody like Putin has them, the only way we can cope with that is by saying, If you use them, so will we. And that has to be a believable threat.

This is actually a different issue from engagement

versus isolation: it is a question of making sure Putin understands that the use of nuclear weapons is totally unacceptable and that if he does use them, he will pay a huge price. That's it. It's not a nice solution. It's not a sort of solution that most Canadians or Americans feel happy with, or most human beings, for that matter, but that's the reality. There isn't another solution. Engaging Putin does not stop him from using his nuclear arsenal—only deterrence does.

RUDYARD GRIFFITHS: In that context, are you concerned about NATO's credibility? Do you think that Putin will test Article 5 of NATO—that says that an attack on one of them is an attack on all of them—somewhere in the Baltic States? If NATO didn't enforce Article 5, how would this affect Putin's larger feelings about deterrence on the nuclear front?

ANNE APPLEBAUM: Putin is already testing NATO. He kidnapped an Estonian officer. He captured a Lithuanian ship. He just conducted an enormous military exercise in the Arctic, which tested Canada. He sends these nuclear bombers to kind of buzz around British airspace. That's what he is doing now. It's a test of NATO and he is gauging our responses. Are we taking him seriously? Do Swedish planes scramble when he flies over Sweden? He is testing us all the time. He is looking to find out how weak or strong NATO threats are, and how far he can push us. It could be extremely dangerous for us not to take him seriously.

RUDYARD GRIFFITHS: Should NATO membership be extended to Ukraine at the appropriate time?

ANNE APPLEBAUM: First of all, that's not a question. It was turned down in 2009 and is not on the table now. It's not going to be on the table anytime soon. It's an irrelevance that keeps coming into the conversation. My more fundamental concern is whether we are sure we can defend existing NATO members. Can we defend the Baltic States? Are we ready to defend Poland or Canada in cases of incursions from the Arctic? Let's think about it. We need to make sure that what we already have is defendable. Remember that since NATO enlargement there has been a Western assumption that there would never really be a Russian threat again. And actually, the whole time NATO was enlarging as an institution, the U.S. and others were building down their forces. In 2013, there were no U.S. tanks in Europe — the Americans took them all out. But American tanks are now back in Europe as of a few weeks ago because people are afraid again.

But we have been building down. We have been pulling out. We never even put NATO bases in eastern Europe. We never moved them anywhere east at the time of expansion, and those are all policies we now need to rethink.

RUDYARD GRIFFITHS: Anne Applebaum, always insightful. We look forward to hearing you at the debate tonight.

ANNE APPLEBAUM: Thank you.

GARRY KASPAROV IN CONVERSATION
WITH RUDYARD GRIFFITHS

RUDYARD GRIFFITHS: Speaking against the motion tonight is Garry Kasparov, well known in the world of chess. More importantly, this is a man who has acted as a dissident in his own country of Russia. He has helped lead a political opposition, both in Russia and abroad, to the regime of Vladimir Putin. He is the chair of the Human Rights Foundation, among his many accolades and hats that he wears today. Garry, great to have you in Toronto.

GARRY KASPAROV: Thanks for inviting me.

RUDYARD GRIFFITHS: Tell us, what is the mood in Russia like? How are average Russians looking at what we are going to debate this evening in Toronto? If this debate were going to take place in downtown Moscow, how would that conversation unfold?

GARRY KASPAROV: If this debate had the chance of taking place in downtown Moscow, I have a feeling my country-men would act very differently. Russia didn't have any meaningful debates for many years. Russia doesn't have live television, so everything is pre-recorded. The very idea of debate could change a lot. Because today, average Russians are swarmed by this 24/7 propaganda that has been seeding hatred for every neighbour of Russia, for the rest of the world, and has created an image of Vladimir Putin as the saviour of Russia from endless enemies.

RUDYARD GRIFFITHS: Are you concerned that by being so critical of Putin — critical of the current Russian regime — you are playing into that propaganda? You are, in a sense, exhibit A for the negative critique of Russia abroad, to the degree that Russia isn't being respected or acknowledged as a proper global power.

GARRY KASPAROV: Look, I have been advocating for the West's engagement with Russia, which is my country, but I believe that Putin's regime is the greatest enemy for the future of Russia. And I am fighting Putin's regime. I don't feel very comfortable arguing against engagement and for isolation today. For me, it's more about appeasement versus containment. Putin's regime is a virus and you don't engage a virus. Russia threatens every neighbour-ing country. But also by his brazen actions in Crimea, Ukraine, and Georgia, Putin has created a very different international atmosphere, one that could jeopardize the entire global order.

RUDYARD GRIFFITHS: Your opponents tonight are probably going to bring up some examples where Russians have been constructive. They have been productive as part of the P5+1 in terms of negotiations with Iran, offering to take the enriched uranium from Iran to Russia and control its release back to Iran. Let's face it; they got Obama out of some hot water in Syria over his red line and chemical weapons.

How do you synch those examples of Russia acting in a broader interest? Or maybe you don't think they have been, with your staunch critique of Mr. Putin and his regime?

GARRY KASPAROV: The two cases that you mentioned definitely play straight into Putin's hands, because a dictator's logic is different from the logic of a democratic president or prime minister. It is all about surviving. They pursue activities that allow them to maintain their grip on power.

Russia was delighted to play this pivotal role in negotiations with Iran. By the way, the negotiation was endless and it helped to maintain the tension in the Middle East, and to keep oil prices quite high. But also, Russia is indispensable now. So that is another bargaining chip for Putin.

Now, as for Syria, Putin always wanted Bashar al-Assad to survive because a new government in Syria could potentially mean that parts of Iraq could become very unstable. The gas from the Gulf could ultimately go to Europe, which would jeopardize Putin's grip on power via the pipeline. With a Russian gas supply, he can hold Europeans hostage.

RUDYARD GRIFFITHS: Do you think low energy prices globally are going to be the best solution to bringing Putin's regime to heel, forcing it to compromise and engage? Or do you think he has a strategy that is going to allow him to dodge that issue?

GARRY KASPAROV: The low energy prices definitely help to curb the dangerous ambitions of Putin's regime. But let's not forget it's a one-man dictatorship. This is not a regime that will be looking for compromise. So that is why we should look for a more combined approach to make sure that people surrounding Putin, including the Russian bureaucracy and middle class, recognize the evils of Putin's rule. That is our best hope. Moreover, it could strengthen the very existence of humanity, because unlike dictators of the past, Putin has his fingertips on the nuclear button.

RUDYARD GRIFFITHS: But is what comes after Putin worse? Should we be careful what we wish for?

GARRY KASPAROV: Putin has been in power for so long that he has succeeded in eliminating decent opposition. In order to stay in power, he has eliminated elections, public debate, and all democratic procedures. He has definitely created an atmosphere that is quite alien to democracy. But the problem is that every day he stays in power, he makes the outcome for the future worse. I wish I could tell you that if Putin left today Russia would be a democracy, but that would be a mistake. And I wouldn't be honest with myself.

If he stays in power one more year, there will be more blood. There will be more tragic events, and eventually there will be less of a chance for Russia to remain in one piece as a state within its current borders, and to recover.

RUDYARD GRIFFITHS: Another thing that is sure to come up tonight is the whole question of NATO's involvement in this crisis, both as a potential bulwark against any tendency Putin might have to expand his ambitions beyond Ukraine and the Baltic States, but also — as Stephen F. Cohen and Vladimir Pozner will likely say — in the sense that we brought this upon ourselves. We didn't treat Russia with respect after the collapse of the Soviet Union. We deployed NATO troops right up to the Russian homeland, and all of this is a reaction to our provocation.

GARRY KASPAROV: There is a difference between invading other countries and understanding the intentions of your potential enemies. This argument falls flat because it means that we do not believe that a hundred million eastern Europeans have the right to decide how they should build their lives or determine what kind of political or economic affiliations they would like to see for their countries. I think that goes against the mentality of the twenty-first century. We are not living in the nineteenth or twentieth centuries. Also, when we look at the facts, NATO expansion was very much on paper. By the year 2013, there was not a single American tank unit in Europe. How can you invade anybody with no tanks?

We also understand the history and read about it in books, but for Baltic nations and Estonians, this is not merely the past—it's a reality. The Baltic nations were always suspicious of Russia, so we have to give them credit. They had rights and a genetic fear of a potential Russian invasion. And unfortunately, Putin's actions have created a lot of unease. They don't forget the invasion of Georgia.

And look at Ukraine. Only about 15 to 17 percent of the country's citizens were NATO sympathizers, mainly people living in the western part. Ukraine and Georgia were flatly denied NATO membership in 2009. Today, you have two-thirds or more of Ukrainians supporting NATO membership. Why? Because they saw what could happen if their country remains defenceless against a powerful neighbour.

RUDYARD GRIFFITHS: Your opponents tonight will probably use Kosovo as an example to respond to Georgia and say, Look, NATO forced the partition of Serbia, and the independence of Kosovo through the bombing of Serbia. Why did NATO get to do that, led by the United States, whereas Russia doesn't get to do the same in Crimea?

GARRY KASPAROV: The partition of Yugoslavia involved many countries. There was a general consensus that this was the right thing to do, based on facts accumulated over years about potential genocide. Europe did not want to see that continue. We should not forget that the partitioning of Yugoslavia has given us seven republics, including Kosovo.

It would be intellectually dishonest to say that every border that was created is perfect. It's the same with the Soviet Union. But the only way to avoid massive bloodshed is to accept these borders. The best way to move forward is to co-operate and find a way for all of these countries to join the European Union, or at least play by the rules to encourage co-operation. Russia acted unilaterally in Georgia. And it was an invasion that had no grounds because there was not a genocide or a potential threat. What is happening in Crimea is the exact opposite of what happened in Kosovo.

RUDYARD GRIFFITHS: And finally, where do you think this tension between East and West goes from here? Are we into the early phases of an extended kind of Cold War? Or is this something that could resolve itself sooner rather than later?

GARRY KASPAROV: Something you just said caught my attention; you said East and West, which was the Cold War. Today, we are no longer dealing with East and West. Who is this East? Russia? Even Ukraine is now fighting Russian invasion. So it is no longer the same lines dividing the world like the Berlin Wall. We now have guys — including Putin — who are fighting the very core values of the free world. The North Korean family dictatorship, ISIS, al Qaeda, and the Venezuelan dictatorship would also fit into this category.

So it is a much broader picture, and it doesn't necessarily have the same geographical division as before. A huge success of global democracy is that Russian is still the dominant language in many of the eastern European nations, including Ukraine. Ethnic Russians living in Ukraine are now fighting and willing to die to secure their right to live in the free world. This is the future I want to see. I believe that many Russians on the other side of the Ukrainian border will eventually have the same desires as Ukrainians. And then I will be the happiest man to talk about the engagement of my country. I want to make sure that the great culture of Russia, including science and other important traditions, will be able to benefit everybody on the planet.

RUDYARD GRIFFITHS: Great. Well, Garry, that is an optimistic note for us to end on. We look forward to hearing more from you in the debate tonight. Thank you for coming to Toronto.

STEPHEN F. COHEN IN CONVERSATION
WITH RUDYARD GRIFFITHS

RUDYARD GRIFFITHS: Stephen F. Cohen, the celebrated American scholar of Soviet and post-Soviet Russia, is with me now. He is also a contributing editor at *The Nation* magazine. Stephen, great to have you in Toronto.

STEPHEN F. COHEN: I don't think anybody has ever called me celebrated.

RUDYARD GRIFFITHS: Well, I certainly would, based on the books you've published.

STEPHEN F. COHEN: There are a lot of adjectives floating around about me, but "celebrated" I have not heard yet. Thank you for having me.

RUDYARD GRIFFITHS: Well, you are celebrated here in Canada.

Let's talk about tonight's debate. The audience is no doubt going to hear from your opponents that the actions of this regime are beyond the pale and that the world should respond aggressively and assertively to Russian actions in Crimea and eastern Ukraine. How do you respond to their hardline stance?

STEPHEN F. COHEN: It's beyond hardline—it's reckless. To respond to this crisis, which was created by the West— not Russia—would flirt with nuclear war. The Russians have made this clear. This is the first time I have heard that kind of talk since the Cuban Missile Crisis, and I have been around for a long time. So that tells us where we're at right now.

The Putin regime, as it has been referred to, has been preposterously demonized in the West, particularly in the United States. I think they are a little calmer about him in Europe, with the exception of maybe in Poland, or half of Poland, I should say. The regime in Moscow is not monstrous; this is a traditional Russian regime. Anybody who thinks that the Putin regime is beyond the pale evidently came to adulthood during the Gorbachev period—the only period of real democratization in Russia. Ms. Applebaum and Mr. Kasparov were born in and lived through the Soviet period, so why would they think this regime is beyond the pale? This is something they have conjured up out of their own misreading of history, and their own ideology. Mr. Kasparov likely has resentments, which I understand, because he is a Russian. He is a very disappointed man. Things in Russia didn't go the way he thought they would in the 1990s.

But I think any rational person understands that the crisis in Ukraine, which is mainly what we're talking about, though there are other resentments against Putin, is something that both Russia and the West are responsible for. And that means that if both sides are responsible, there is territory to negotiate this crisis. But my opponents don't want to negotiate. If we follow the logic of what they say, it sounds like they want to go to war; it's almost as though they want a showdown — military or otherwise — with this hated Putin. That worries me, because we should not be thinking about conflict in the world today in such a way.

RUDYARD GRIFFITHS: How do you see that showdown potentially happening? Is this about the Baltic States? Is it about the situation in Ukraine right now? Or is it something else entirely?

STEPHEN F. COHEN: So as far as I can empirically tell, Russia represents no threat to the Baltic States whatsoever. This notion that somehow Ukraine is also about the Baltics was conjured up by those members of NATO that have wanted to move front-line, permanent NATO military infrastructure and bases to the Baltics right on Russia's borders for fifteen years, but have been prohibited from doing so by an agreement with Russia. The West signed an agreement when NATO was expanded that there would be no such bases that close to Russia.

And we know who these people are, and what countries

they live in. We can name names; it's not a secret. The three Baltic countries themselves would love to have NATO bases; everybody wants NATO bases. It's great for the economy — you don't have to pay for your own defence, since lots of Americans come and spend money. Merchants do well. It's a windfall, but it's reckless militarily. However, the Baltics, Poland, and now Sweden, which is not a member of NATO, all want NATO's protection. There is a strong faction in Sweden that wants to be a member of NATO so that they can show that the threat to the Baltics is real, because it's kind of hard to demonstrate right now.

Remember when they thought they saw a submarine in the lagoon and never found it? They are running these fictitious threat operations that the Russians are coming, but it simply isn't true. Now Ukraine is horribly serious. It's a new Cold War right on Russia's borders. So what sort of bad resolution do I see here? I think it could be some kind of war between the United States, NATO, and Russia.

There is very strong pressure on President Obama to send three billion dollars' worth of weapons to Kiev to fight against the Russian-backed rebels in the east. Ukraine has no army; it has been defeated twice by rebels, so it is not clear who would use these weapons — probably the battalions. But the battalions are ultra nationalist, ideological fighters, and I'm not sure you want to give them weapons.

But Moscow perceives this escalation of arming Kiev as requiring a military response. Well, what would that military response be? If you read the Russian press, the generals are telling Putin if the Ukrainian military is rebuilt and rearmed to that degree, the defensible front line where the ceasefire is now is essentially no longer defensible. So they are saying to Putin: Mr. President, we need to help the rebels extend their defensible front line, at a minimum because it's on the sea. And they would have the seaport.

The West would have to react to that action. So I'm guessing NATO would enter western Ukraine. So you now have NATO—the United States, in effect—paying and leading an occupation in Ukraine. It's the Cuban Missile Crisis.

RUDYARD GRIFFITHS: The analogies of World War II are going to be brought up in this debate. People are going to say that this isn't about isolation versus engagement. This is about appeasement versus containment. Anne Applebaum and Gary Kasparov are on the containment side; you're arguing for appeasement.

STEPHEN F. COHEN: No, I'm arguing for détente. We have been through this before. We went through it with the Soviet Union. I was on a committee in the United States formed by CEOs of American corporations, big ones— IBM companies and PepsiCo. They wanted to trade with the Soviet Union and understood that trade required some kind of political buffer. We can't constantly be getting so furious that we would resort to sanctions as we did back then.

And détente ultimately triumphed after a lot of defeats because Ronald Reagan, of all people, embraced it. And he and Gorbachev both thought, wrongly as it turns out, that they had ended the Cold War forever.

People who talk about appeasement and reference the analogy of Munich and Hitler make me think their brains froze in 1938. Can't they think of some other historical analogy? This is a serious history. It's not serious political analysis and it's reckless foreign policy making. Putin is not expansive. He's not Hitler, and it's not clear what our political leaders think. But we know one thing: the chancellor of Germany, Angela Merkel, and the president of France, François Hollande, went into an absolute panic in February when they realized that the Americans were serious about arming Kiev.

RUDYARD GRIFFITHS: John McCain.

STEPHEN F. COHEN: They thought it was just typical American rhetoric, that we talk a lot and we don't do anything. And normally that is what we do. But they became convinced that it was going to happen and then flew quickly to Minsk and Washington, and all these other places, to sign the Minsk Accord.

Now Poroshenko, the president of Ukraine, signed it a few days ago, and then violated it by passing some laws that are completely contrary to what he signed. Merkel and Hollande are absolutely furious. But it is now political, if you see what I mean. We are now at the tipping point. All the parties involved have a chance to negotiate. The people who seem to want a showdown with Russia are the enemies of this agreement. They are very powerful and they are represented at your debate here in Toronto tonight. I don't know how two grown-ups who have as much knowledge as our opponents have, and have lived the lives they have could work themselves into this really irrational anger about Putin.

RUDYARD GRIFFITHS: Finally, talk to us about why you think there is a faction out there that wants this showdown. As you mentioned, nuclear weapons are involved here, so the risk seems very high. Where does this come from? What is the agenda that is pushing your opponents forward here?

STEPHEN F. COHEN: I don't want to talk about Ms. Applebaum and Mr. Kasparov because I don't know how they've talked themselves into this position. Everybody has an autobiography: Kasparov was once a Soviet hero. He was a legendary figure in the Soviet Union. Although he is not Russian by origin, he's culturally Russian. And Applebaum is a very eminent figure with a long history of writing about Russia.

You asked me how I know there are people who want a showdown with Putin even if it involves the military. Because they say so. They talk about weapons being defensive, not offensive. I have no idea what a defensive weapon is, unless it is a tank cannon that can only shoot in one direction or a rifle without bullets — it's nonsense, and everybody knows it. They want to escalate what is already a military crisis. And for what purpose? They think this will result in a defeat of Putin's leadership and that he will just go away.

Kasparov said the other day, for example, that Putin is a cancer and, as with any cancer, you have to cut it out. Actually, medically that's not true; many cancers are not cut out and treated. But to carry his metaphor forward, he means that Putin's regime has to be removed by one means or another. If he were sitting here, I would ask Garry if he thought we should use NATO military action to remove Putin, and I'm sure he would say that if it's possible then why not.

Applebaum has a different view, I think. My understanding is that she really believes Putin is somehow on the march and that if he prevails in Ukraine, he will hit elsewhere. But the showdown is in their minds. It certainly is in Senator McCain's mind and the minds of the entire United States Congress. In both houses — in four votes over four or five months — only forty-eight members of the House voted against condemning Putin's actions. No members of the Senate. There is no substantial political opposition on this topic in the United States. So it's not just McCain who seems to want a showdown with Putin — it's all of Washington.

RUDYARD GRIFFITHS: Well, that is a sombre note to end on here, and on which to start what should be a fabulous debate this evening.

STEPHEN F. COHEN: To defend my own country, I hear that

this point of view is quite strong in Canada as well. But since I don't live here I can't say that first-hand.

RUDYARD GRIFFITHS: You will get a definite flavour for it tonight. Stephen F. Cohen, thank you for coming to Toronto to be part of this debate.

STEPHEN F. COHEN: Thanks for having me.

VLADIMIR POZNER IN CONVERSATION
WITH RUDYARD GRIFFITHS

RUDYARD GRIFFITHS: I am joined by Vladimir Pozner, who will be arguing for the resolution tonight. He is an Emmy Award–winning journalist and host of the top-rated Russian current affairs show on Channel One, as well as a bestselling author. Vladimir, great to have you here in Toronto.

VLADIMIR POZNER: It is my pleasure.

RUDYARD GRIFFITHS: You've had a lifetime of engagement with this relationship between the Western world and Russia, sometimes good and sometimes bad. Where are we at right now? Are we at the beginnings of a new Cold War?

VLADIMIR POZNER: The answer to that is yes and no because

the Cold War was really based on ideology. Two systems were fighting each other, each one believing that it was right. It wasn't about geopolitics. It was about convincing the other that we have the right system; we have the right ideas; it was also about capitalism versus socialism — or versus communism — depending on how you look at it. That was the Cold War, and that is not happening now.

It is a different situation now, but it is just as dangerous — perhaps even more dangerous. At this point it's a propaganda war — a media war — about geopolitical interests. It's about whether or not a country feels threatened. Rightly or wrongly, Russia feels threatened by NATO. And it's about whether or not the United States is concerned about nuclear weapons. Because back in the Cold War days, the Americans were very fearful of nuclear weapons, and I think MAD played a key role in preventing war. Kids were taught to hide under desks. There were movies like *The Day After*. People were very much aware of it. I don't think it's the same today. Somehow, the whole issue of nuclear war has kind of dissolved. And I think that's dangerous.

RUDYARD GRIFFITHS: Tonight you are putting forward the argument that the West should be engaging Russia not isolating it. Are you concerned about a nuclear threat here, or that a set of errors could happen if the West pursued a policy of isolation, or even something more hardline, against Russia?

VLADIMIR POZNER: I am very concerned, especially because

to whose advantage is it really to isolate Russia? Who wins from that? And my argument is going to be that isolation makes countries worse off. The Soviet Union is a good example of that. Non-recognition and isolation allowed Stalin to do things that he would not have been able to do had there been engagement. And I want to make it very clear that engagement and appeasement are not at all the same thing.

RUDYARD GRIFFITHS: Look at the relationship today from the lens of what's happening in Ukraine. I'm sure your opponents tonight are going to say that the global community can't support the Russian actions first in Crimea and now in the eastern regions of Ukraine. Russia has behaved in such a way that it has in fact labelled itself as a rogue state, and it should be treated as such. How are you going to respond to that line of criticism?

VLADIMIR POZNER: Well, if that line of thinking does come up, I would say that, first of all, Russia sees what is happening in Ukraine as a threat. It sees Ukraine becoming a member of NATO in the future, meaning that NATO would be on Russia's southwestern border. And in the case of Crimea, had Crimea remained in Ukraine, its most important naval base, in Sevastopol, could have become a NATO or American naval base.

It sees all of this as a threat. Look back to 1962, when the United States did not allow the Soviet Union to base its missiles in Cuba, although the two countries had agreed to do it. The U.S. didn't have jurisdiction in the area, but it said it wouldn't permit the missiles nonetheless. The country threatened to sink the Soviet fleet because officials viewed the actions as a threat to their national security and thought, to hell with international law.

It's pretty much the same thing today. I don't think any of this would have happened if there had been some kind of guarantee that Ukraine would not become a member of NATO for the next thirty years. I think there is a real fear of NATO in Russia. Why does it exist now? There is no more Soviet Union; there is no Warsaw Pact. Who is NATO being used against? Who is the threat? If it's Russia, then come out and say so. But they're saying, Well, it's about North Korea and Iran, and you know people don't bite.

I want to make this very clear. I am not a Putin supporter at all. I think that some of the things that were done were completely wrong, but that doesn't change my attitude about engagement. If you don't engage, more of this is going to happen. On the other hand, you have examples like Kosovo. NATO bombed Yugoslavia but nobody allowed it, not even the UN. Kosovars, who had always been part of Serbia, suddenly became independent, and everybody started saying, That's fine, but then why can't others do the same thing?

The world has come to a point where might actually means right. Whoever is the strongest does whatever it wants. And today, the United States is the eight-hundred-pound gorilla, there is no doubt about that. And Russia is very concerned, correctly or incorrectly.

RUDYARD GRIFFITHS: Talk to us about how the average Russian is looking at this situation. Is this feeling registering not just in the Kremlin, but also on the streets of towns and cities across Russia?

VLADIMIR POZNER: Of course. This has also been part of the propaganda. The major television outlets in Russia, the so-called federal channels, are either owned and operated, or just operated, by the government. And so the picture that people get of the world and what's happening inside the country is a Kremlin-organized picture. That is the definition of propaganda, and it's pretty effective.

But people are not stupid. Remember what Lincoln said: "You can fool some of the people but you can't fool them all the time." Reaction to this propaganda probably would have been different if the Russian people didn't also have the feeling that the West kind of had it in for Russia; they said, You lost the Cold War. Shut up. Go back into your cave. You're a second-rate power and we don't care about you. It would have likely been different if there hadn't been that feeling of being disrespected and disregarded as a great nation.

Today, anti-Americanism in Russia is far higher than during the Cold War. Anti-Americanism used to be against the American government and the American system — today it's against Americans. They are seen as the enemy. And on the other side of the equation, you have over 80 percent of Russians supporting Putin. That poll was conducted by a very respectable independent organization called the Levada-Centre.

RUDYARD GRIFFITHS: And finally, where does this conflict go from here. Let's say you're right. And let's say the West can find its way through to a new "engagement" with Russia. What would that look like? And are you optimistic that it could bear some results in the immediate or near future?

VLADIMIR POZNER: I'm not optimistic. I don't think it can happen while Obama is president of the United States, because it would mean loss of face, among other things. I don't think it can happen when Putin's the president of Russia, because there is a profound distrust of him as a leader. He basically says you can't trust the Americans. So I would be optimistic if there were a change in leadership in both countries. I think that would be the key to real change. Otherwise it's going to be very slow and difficult. And as I said, I'm not optimistic. Maybe there is light at the end of the tunnel, but I'll tell you what, it's a heck of a long tunnel.

RUDYARD GRIFFITHS: We know that there is going to be a change in leadership in the United States in 2016. We're not so sure about Russia.

VLADIMIR POZNER: We are pretty sure there won't be. That's the fact. He is playing his cards very close to his chest, as they say in poker. I mean, he's not saying if he is going to run or not, but people feel that he will. In addition to that, sadly enough, there is no one else to turn to, as far as most people are concerned. The leader of the Communist party? That's a joke. The leader of the so-called Just Russia party is even more of a joke. The leader of the Liberal Democrats is a clown, so there is nobody there. And the democratic opposition — the real opposition — has never been able to come together as allies and stand as a unified group.

So everyone is in his little corner with no options around. And, of course, a lot of people would say Putin has made sure that there would be nobody out there. I'd say yes and no. He has brought Russia back. Now you have to contend with Russia. You can't just ignore her. So I am not optimistic, no.

RUDYARD GRIFFITHS: Vladimir Pozner, we are going to leave it there, but you have got a great debate set for you tonight. Thank you for coming from Moscow directly to participate in this debate. It's great to have you here in Canada.

VLADIMIR POZNER: Thank you so much.

Post-Debate Commentary

POST-DEBATE COMMENTARY BY
EDWARD GREENSPON

Russia has long perplexed the North Atlantic alliance, not to mention its neighbours. To hear Vladimir Pozner tell it, the current angst in the West over whether and how to isolate Vladimir Putin's Russia for its Ukrainian transgressions is not only wrong-headed but part of a continuum of wrong-headedness dating back to at least the 1917 Bolshevik Revolution, which was followed by failed Western military expeditions against the newborn communist state.

The issue of whether the West has been too antagonistic toward Russia, or too accommodating, was one of several lively debates within the greater Munk Debate on Friday, April 10, at Toronto's Roy Thomson Hall. The question put to the debaters—Cold War–era commentator Pozner and U.S. academic Stephen F. Cohen for the pro side and journalist Anne Applebaum and dissident chess great Garry Kasparov on the con—was "Be it resolved the West should engage not isolate Russia." The fact that the live audience of 3,000 ended the evening split 48 percent to 52 percent speaks to the complexity of the riddle of what to do about Russia.

The debates-within-the-debate variously touched upon who, if anyone, should be isolated: Putin or Russia? If the West is actually doing more to harm its own national security interests by treating Russia as a pariah rather than a partner in bigger struggles, such as against Islamic extremists; did the West bring this upon itself through aggressive NATO expansion; and should it have been guided, as it was, by the security wishes of the sovereign nations of the former East bloc or the traditional sphere of influence claimed by Russia.

For Cohen and Pozner, the issue very much boiled down to "Who lost Russia"—their answer being successive U.S. administrations. By disrespecting its former Cold War adversary in the years following the 1991 breakup of the Soviet Union, the U.S., in particular, created the conditions for Putinism. The trick for them is to stop making the same mistake. They argued that a) Russia cannot be isolated in today's globalized world, and b) it would be folly to turn against a front-line partner in the fight against greater threats. "The demonization of Vladimir Putin is not a policy," Cohen declared, quoting Kissinger before taking it one step further and suggesting that "the demonization of Putin is an excuse to abandon analysis."

Kasparov and Applebaum thoroughly rejected the assertion that the West humiliated and excluded 1990s

Russia, observing it invited its former nemesis into such elite councils as the G8, WTO, and Council of Europe. For the cons, the issue at hand is very much Putin, who they characterized as a mafia-like figure operating a corrupt kleptocracy that leans on anti-American propaganda to shore up its domestic political position. (Bertolt Brecht's anti-Nazi satire, *The Resistible Rise of Arturo Ui*, comes to mind.) Kasparov argued Putin has no policy other than maintaining power. "In chess we have fixed rules and unpredictable results," he said. "Putin's Russia is the exact opposite."

The Ukrainian crisis was nothing more than a reaction against a movement that, in the words of Applebaum, was "fighting oligarchs, corruption, and Putinism." It was not, as Cohen and Pozner contended, the natural by-product of a Russia that felt threatened by NATO expansion and is now basking in its re-emergence as a power to reckon with.

Both sides agreed the issues at hand have splintered the Western alliance. Cohen excoriated Western policy for fixating on Putin rather than pursuing its own broader interests. Applebaum blamed the divisions on the corrupting effect of Putin being allowed to pour his ill-gotten financial gains into European politics.

Kasparov, famous for an aggressive, freewheeling approach to chess, set himself up for the greatest come-uppance of the evening, demanding of Pozner: "When was the last time you were in Kiev?" Pozner looked up and curtly replied he'd been there two years ago to accept an award as Ukraine's Man of the Year. In case anyone missed it, Cohen stuck the knife in further. "I hope you noticed that the chess master just got checkmated."

Kasparov seemed to withdraw from the field of combat for a short period. Perhaps he needed time to examine the board and contemplate the moves open to him. Soon enough, though, he was back in the mix, retorting belatedly but effectively that two years previously, the pro-Russian Viktor Yanukovych had presided over the Ukraine that made Pozner its Man of the Year.

As the debate went into its late innings, Cohen kept returning to the themes that the U.S. had misjudged Putin (he was on his knees pleading to be part of the West) and that U.S. policy shouldn't be about punishing Putin but serving its own national interest. Striking the pose of the classic realist, he mocked Applebaum for her fairy tales. The U.S. and its allies, he said, had created a situation today more dangerous than during the Cold War, when there were at least protocols about how the superpowers interacted, including the famed hotline between the Kremlin and the White House.

Now it was time for Applebaum to turn the tables on the self-styled realists, accusing them of pining for the good old days of Cold War Russia, when they could simply divide up their bipolar world. Engagement with whom, she challenged, cutting to the crux of the dilemma embedded in the phrase "Putin's Russia." Is Western policy to isolate Putin? Or Russia? Can the two be separated, as sanctions, weak though they are, attempt to do? Can one be defeated without the other? Is Putin's Russia a unique creature, as the cons would have it, or the natural extension of the czars' Russia, Stalin's Russia, Breshnev's Russia?

The big elephant in the room was barely addressed by the debaters: How could Western leaders use statecraft to discourage Putin from further territorial incursions, and what to do if he were to take his Ukraine playbook to the Baltics, which are NATO members and therefore protected in law by the famous Article 5 that says an armed attack against one member is an attack against all. Answers were not readily forthcoming.

If you are on the side of using isolation as a lever, it is particularly incumbent upon you to identity policies that will be effective and can win support across a divided alliance. Perhaps that's why the con side won the most audience applause by far but barely prevailed with 52 percent of the vote (up ten points from the pre-debate tally).

By the same token, if you favour engagement, what's your strategy in the face of blatant and repeated assaults on sovereign nations?

I spent the years 1988 to 1991 covering the collapse of the Soviet Empire and the restoration of independence among its client states in central and eastern Europe. On my first visit to Russia with a university group in 1985, several of us met a couple of fellow students in Leningrad who invited us back to their place to listen to underground music and talk about our differing worlds. Gorbachev had recently been named general secretary and we had a *Time* magazine with his face on the cover. Our hosts initially could not believe the strawberry blotch on his forehead hadn't been airbrushed in by Western propagandists rather than airbrushed out by their own.

It happened to be my birthday, and I can easily recall the poignancy of the night as one of the Russian students sadly explained how he wanted to be a graphic artist but the state had determined a different course for him. He was clearly also struggling with his sexual identity, and the conversation carried a subtext about the impossibility of being a gay man in Soviet Russia (a theme recurring in Putin's Russia).

In my time covering political change in Poland, Romania, East Germany, Hungary, Ukraine, and Russia, I was reminded over and over of the universality of the urge for personal freedom.

With all that in mind, I was struck by a plaintive comment from Kasparov in the late stages of the debate. He was still in his twenties when the Soviet Union collapsed. He commented on how he remembered when he didn't have freedom and the feeling when freedom arrived. Now freedom was slipping away again in Putin's Russia. "I want to see my country free and strong," he said.

Whatever the failures in policy, therein lies the real tragedy of the situation.

Edward Greenspon is a journalist who has reported from Russia and Ukraine during his career. He was most recently in Moscow in February.

POST-DEBATE COMMENTARY BY STEVE PAIKIN

It's been almost a quarter century since the world watched in astonishment as the old hammer and sickle red flag of the Soviet Union descended from the Kremlin's flagpole and was replaced by the Russian tricolour. For a while, it appeared as if the West and Russia might establish a new, unprecedented co-operative relationship.

Times, as they always do in international affairs, have changed dramatically. We seem to be in the midst of a new Cold War with Russia, all of which made for important fodder for the latest Munk Debate at Roy Thomson Hall last Friday night. It was the fifteenth such debate in a series that has brought together the brightest minds and sharpest thinkers. This evening's participants were former Soviet broadcaster Vladimir Pozner and New York University Russian studies professor Stephen F. Cohen, who argued that *more engagement* with Russia will ensure a more secure West. Former chess champion Garry

Kasparov and author/journalist Anne Applebaum urged *more isolation* and a tougher line against rogue dictator Vladimir Putin.

"Isolating any country is not only counterproductive but dangerous, especially if the country is as big, as wealthy, as powerful, and as unpredictable as Russia," warned Pozner, who seemed to blame a lack of recognition and engagement by the West for the Soviet system developing as it did, and for the millions of starving Ukrainians and the Soviet occupation of eastern Europe. To the astonishment of his debate opponents, Pozner insisted that if the West's policy hadn't been aimed at humbling a nation of proud people, Russia would be a different country today.

Russia's current leaders *own the nation*, countered Applebaum. They control everything through "theft, graft, and money laundering." She explained that 110 people control 35 percent of the country's wealth, essentially making it a mafia state. We must make Putin pay a high price so he doesn't invade another neighbour, she declared.

Stephen F. Cohen admonished his opponents by quoting former New York senator Daniel Patrick Moynihan: "You're entitled to your own opinions, but you're not entitled to your own facts." "These are the facts," Cohen proceeded. "In this globalized world, it is impossible to isolate Russia. Russia is too big, too rich, too interconnected."

Cohen noted that even with the West's deteriorating relationship with Russia, Putin has signed more economic, political, and military agreements with the rest of the world than America has. Isolating Russia hasn't made them more compliant, it's made them turn elsewhere, he said. A further destabilized Russia will be worse.

Kasparov, who lives "in exile" in Manhattan, spoke of his "dream" coming true in 1991, when the Soviet Union died without any of the bloodshed seen in the Balkans with the disintegration of the former Yugoslavia. The West invested billions of dollars in Russia. And then Putin came in, restored the old Soviet national anthem, and turned the country into a one-man dictatorship, he said. Kasparov tried his hand at politics but found the deck completely stacked against his opposition forces, who were denied access to media and fundraising. "In chess we have fixed rules and an unpredictable result," he said. "In Putin's Russia, it's the exact opposite."

Henry Kissinger wrote that the demonizing of Putin is not a policy, argued Cohen.

Applebaum countered that the West tried engagement and it hasn't worked. "Presidents Clinton and Bush invited Russia to join the G8," she said, noting that we did engage and invite Russia into our institutions and their response was to invade Chechnya, Georgia, and Ukraine.

Kasparov wanted to come back to an earlier point. "This is the first time I've heard someone suggest that a policy of engagement in the 1920s could have prevented Stalinist terror," he said incredulously. "Lenin said, 'We'll treat the West as useful idiots who'll sell us the very rope that we'll use to hang them.'"

As in most Munk Debates, there were also moments of comedy, even though the topic was deadly serious. As Kasparov's temperature rose and he became more and more animated, Pozner asked, "Why are you yelling at me?"

"That's how he always talks," said Applebaum.

"Because I am also Russian," replied Kasparov.

Comic relief aside, Applebaum went on to describe Russia as a virulently anti-American country, thanks to a non-stop bombardment of anti-American propaganda in the Russian media.

Cohen wasn't buying: "I read ten Russian newspapers every day," he said, conceding that what Applebaum said was true for three of them, but not for the other seven.

"How many Ukrainian newspapers do you read?" Applebaum shot back.

"I read ten Russian newspapers every day," was all Cohen could muster before turning to another point.

We expanded NATO toward their borders, Cohen continued. "We were continuously warned by liberal Russians—people we liked in Russia—that we were pushing too far."

Central Europeans wanted to be in NATO, said Applebaum. "The United States very reluctantly agreed to expand the security zone so that the people—all 100 million of them—would be able to transition to democracy and begin economic development and growth without fear of invasion. And it worked. It's been unbelievably successful."

But Cohen insisted those moves to include central or eastern European countries in NATO violated an agreement America made with the former Soviet Union.

"James Baker, the then U.S. secretary of state,

expressed to [Gorbachev] that if they agreed to the unification of Germany and took down the Berlin Wall, NATO would not move one inch to the east." Cohen went on to say that the wall did indeed come down—and then America abrogated the agreement by admitting Poland and the Czech Republic into NATO, claiming that the agreement had been with the Soviet Union, not Russia.

Pozner concluded the night with a David Letterman–style Top Ten list of reasons not to isolate Russia, including that it would only embolden the chauvinists, turn Russia toward the East (including China), make Russia more unpredictable, and lead to a new generation of Russians who are hostile to the West.

As with all Munk Debates, the audience of 3,000 was invited to vote twice: once at the beginning of the night, then again after hearing the competing arguments. When the night began, 58 percent agreed that more engagement and less isolation of Russia was the way to go, while 42 percent disagreed. After a spirited debate, only 48 percent wanted more engagement, while 52 percent urged for more isolation. The con side moved more votes, and thus carried another fascinating night at Roy Thomson Hall.

Steve Paikin is anchor of The Agenda with Steve Paikin on *TVO.*

ACKNOWLEDGEMENTS

The Munk Debates are the product of the public-spiritedness of a remarkable group of civic-minded organizations and individuals. First and foremost, these debates would not be possible without the vision and leadership of the Aurea Foundation. Founded in 2006 by Peter and Melanie Munk, the Aurea Foundation supports Canadian individuals and institutions involved in the study and development of public policy. The debates are the foundation's signature initiative, a model for the kind of substantive public policy conversation Canadians can foster globally. Since the creation of the debates in 2008, the foundation has underwritten the entire cost of each semi-annual event. The debates have also benefited from the input and advice of members of the board of the foundation, including Mark Cameron, Andrew Coyne, Devon Cross, Allan Gotlieb, George Jonas, Margaret MacMillan, Anthony Munk, Robert Prichard, and Janice Stein.

For his contribution to the preliminary edit of the book, the debate organizers would like to thank Patrick Luciani.

Since their inception, the Munk Debates have sought to take the discussions that happen at each event to national and international audiences. Here the debates have benefited immeasurably from a partnership with Canada's national newspaper, the *Globe and Mail*, and the counsel of its editor-in-chief, David Walmsley.

With the publication of this superb book, House of Anansi Press is helping the debates reach new audiences in Canada and around the world. The debates' organizers would like to thank Anansi chair Scott Griffin and president and publisher Sarah MacLachlan for their enthusiasm for this book project and insights into how to translate the spoken debate into a powerful written intellectual exchange.

ABOUT THE DEBATERS

VLADIMIR POZNER is a veteran journalist and bestselling author. He is the host of the top-rated weekly current affairs program on Channel One—Russia's largest TV network. Named the "Voice of Moscow" by CNN, he is a regular commentator on Russia and the Cold War in Western media. He is also the author of a number of best-selling books, including *Parting with Illusions* and *Eyewitness: A Personal Account of the Unraveling of the Soviet Union*. Pozner has won multiple awards, including three Emmy certificates and nine TEFY awards. He was also a correspondent for NBC during the 2014 Sochi Olympic Games, and has been a frequent guest on Western media analyzing the conflict in Ukraine and the partition of Crimea.

STEPHEN F. COHEN is professor emeritus of politics and Russian studies at Princeton University and professor emeritus of Russian studies and history at New York

University. He is the author of a number of widely acclaimed books on Russia, including *Bukharin and the Bolshevik Revolution: A Political Biography*; *Rethinking the Soviet Experience*; and, most recently, *Soviet Fates and Lost Alternatives: From Stalinism to the New Cold War*. His new book *Why the Cold War Again?* will be published in 2015. Cohen is also a contributing editor to *The Nation* magazine and his articles have appeared in the *New York Times*, *Washington Post*, and other American and international publications.

ANNE APPLEBAUM is a journalist and leading expert on Russia. She was a member of the editorial board of the *Washington Post* between 2002 and 2006 and her writing has appeared in the *New Yorker* and the *New Republic*, among others. She is the author of several books about central and eastern Europe, including *Gulag: A History*, which won the 2004 Pulitzer Prize for Nonfiction, and *Iron Curtain: The Crushing of Eastern Europe, 1944–1956*, which won the 2013 Cundill Prize in Historical Literature. Both books were nominated for the National Book Award. Her foreign affairs column appears biweekly in the *Washington Post* and *Slate*, and is syndicated around the world. Applebaum is currently the director of the Transitions Forum at the Legatum Institute.

GARRY KASPAROV came to international fame in 1985 as the youngest chess champion ever, at the age of twenty-two. He broke Bobby Fischer's rating record in 1990 and his own peak rating record remained unbroken until

2013. He retired from competitive chess in 2005 to join the vanguard of the Russian pro-democracy movement. He founded the United Civil Front and organized the Marches of Dissent to protest the repressive policies of Vladimir Putin. In 2012, Kasparov was elected to the Coordinating Council of the united opposition movement and named chairman of the New York–based Human Rights Foundation, succeeding Vaclav Havel. Kasparov has been a contributing editor to the *Wall Street Journal* since 1991 and is a frequent commentator on politics and human rights. His book on decision-making, *How Life Imitates Chess*, is available in over twenty languages.

ABOUT THE EDITOR

RUDYARD GRIFFITHS is the chair of the Munk Debates and president of the Aurea Charitable Foundation. In 2006 he was named one of Canada's "Top 40 under 40" by the *Globe and Mail.* He is the editor of thirteen books on history, politics, and international affairs, including *Who We Are: A Citizen's Manifesto,* which was a *Globe and Mail* Best Book of 2009 and a finalist for the Shaughnessy Cohen Prize for Political Writing. He lives in Toronto with his wife and two children.

ABOUT THE MUNK DEBATES

The Munk Debates are Canada's premier public policy event. Held semi-annually, the debates provide leading thinkers with a global forum to discuss the major public policy issues facing the world and Canada. Each event takes place in Toronto in front of a live audience, and the proceedings are covered by domestic and international media. Participants in recent Munk Debates include Robert Bell, Tony Blair, John Bolton, Ian Bremmer, Daniel Cohn-Bendit, Paul Collier, Howard Dean, Hernando de Soto, Alan Dershowitz, Maureen Dowd, Gareth Evans, Mia Farrow, Niall Ferguson, William Frist, Newt Gingrich, David Gratzer, Glenn Greenwald, Michael Hayden, Rick Hillier, Christopher Hitchens, Richard Holbrooke, Josef Joffe, Robert Kagan, Henry Kissinger, Charles Krauthammer, Paul Krugman, Arthur Laffer, Lord Nigel Lawson, Stephen Lewis, David Li, Bjørn Lomborg, Lord Peter Mandelson, Elizabeth May, George Monbiot,

Caitlin Moran, Dambisa Moyo, Vali Nasr, Alexis Ohanian, Camille Paglia, George Papandreou, Samantha Power, David Rosenberg, Hanna Rosin, Anne-Marie Slaughter, Bret Stephens, Lawrence Summers, Amos Yadlin, and Fareed Zakaria.

The Munk Debates are a project of the Aurea Foundation, a charitable organization established in 2006 by philanthropists Peter and Melanie Munk to promote public policy research and discussion. For more information, visit www.munkdebates.com.

ABOUT THE INTERVIEWS

Rudyard Griffiths's interviews with Anne Applebaum, Garry Kasparov, Stephen F. Cohen, and Vladimir Pozner were recorded on April 10, 2015. The Aurea Foundation is gratefully acknowledged for permission to reprint excerpts from the following:

(p. 55) "Anne Applebaum in Conversation," by Rudyard Griffiths. Copyright © 2015 Aurea Foundation. Transcribed by Transcript Divas.

(p. 63) "Garry Kasparov in Conversation," by Rudyard Griffiths. Copyright © 2015 Aurea Foundation. Transcribed by Transcript Divas.

(p. 71) "Stephen F. Cohen in Conversation," by Rudyard Griffiths. Copyright © 2015 Aurea Foundation. Transcribed by Transcript Divas.

ABOUT THE POST-DEBATE COMMENTARY

Edward Greenspon's and Steve Paikin's post-debate commentaries were written following the debates on April 10, 2015. The Aurea Foundation wishes to thank Rudyard Griffiths for his assistance in commissioning these essays.

Has Obama Made the World a More Dangerous Place?

Kagan and Stephens vs. Zakaria and Slaughter

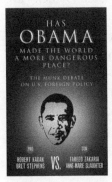

From Ukraine to the Middle East to China, the United States is redefining its role in international affairs. Famed historian and foreign policy commentator Robert Kagan and Pulitzer Prize–winning journalist Bret Stephens take on CNN's Fareed Zakaria and noted academic and political commentator Anne-Marie Slaughter to debate the foreign policy legacy of President Obama.

"Superpowers don't get to retire ... In the international sphere, Americans have had to act as judge, jury, police, and, in the case of military action, executioner." —Robert Kagan

Are Men Obsolete?
Rosin and Dowd vs. Moran and Paglia

For the first time in history, will it be better to be a woman than a man in the upcoming century? Renowned author and editor Hanna Rosin and Pulitzer Prize–winning columnist Maureen Dowd challenge *New York Times*–bestselling author Caitlin Moran and trailblazing social critic Camille Paglia to debate the relative decline of the power and status of men in the workplace, the family, and society at large.

"Feminism was always wrong to pretend women could 'have it all.' It is not male society but Mother Nature who lays the heaviest burden on women." —Camille Paglia

Should We Tax the Rich More?
Krugman and Papandreou vs. Gingrich and Laffer

 Is imposing higher taxes on the wealthy the best way for countries to reinvest in their social safety nets, education, and infrastructure while protecting the middle class? Or does raising taxes on society's wealth creators lead to capital flight, falling government revenues, and less money for the poor? Nobel Prize–winning economist Paul Krugman and former prime minister of Greece George Papandreou square off against former speaker of the U.S. House of Representatives Newt Gingrich and famed economist Arthur Laffer to debate this key issue.

"The effort to finance Big Government through higher taxes is a direct assault on civil society."   —Newt Gingrich

Can the World Tolerate an Iran with Nuclear Weapons?
Krauthammer and Yadlin vs. Zakaria and Nasr

Is the case for a pre-emptive strike on Iran ironclad? Or can a nuclear Iran be a stabilizing force in the Middle East? Former Israel Defense Forces head of military intelligence Amos Yadlin, Pulitzer Prize–winning political commentator Charles Krauthammer, CNN host Fareed Zakaria, and Iranian-born academic Vali Nasr debate the consequences of a nuclear-armed Iran.

"Deterring Iran is fundamentally different from deterring the Soviet Union. You could rely on the latter but not the former."
—Charles Krauthammer

North America's Lost Decade?

Krugman and Rosenberg vs. Summers and Bremmer

The future of the North American economy is more uncertain than ever. In this edition of the Munk Debates, Nobel Prize–winning economist Paul Krugman and chief economist and strategist at Gluskin Sheff + Associates David Rosenberg square off against former U.S. treasury secretary Lawrence Summers and bestselling author Ian Bremmer to tackle the resolution, "Be it resolved: North America faces a Japan-style era of high unemployment and slow growth."

"It's now impossible to deny the obvious, which is that we are not now, and have never been, on the road to recovery."

—Paul Krugman

Hitchens vs. Blair
Christopher Hitchens vs. Tony Blair

Intellectual juggernaut and staunch atheist Christopher Hitchens goes head-to-head with former British prime minister Tony Blair, one of the Western world's most openly devout political leaders, on the age-old question: Is religion a force for good in the world? Few world leaders have had a greater hand in shaping current events than Blair; few writers have been more outspoken and polarizing than Hitchens.

Sharp, provocative, and thoroughly engrossing, *Hitchens vs. Blair* is a rigorous and electrifying intellectual sparring match on the contentious questions that continue to dog the topic of religion in our globalized world.

"If religious instruction were not allowed until the child had attained the age of reason, we would be living in a very different world." —Christopher Hitchens

houseofanansi.com/collections/munk-debates

The Munk Debates: Volume One
Edited by Rudyard Griffiths; Introduction by Peter Munk

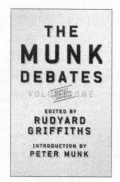

Launched in 2008 by philanthropists Peter and Melanie Munk, the Munk Debates is Canada's premier international debate series, a highly anticipated cultural event that brings together the world's brightest minds.

This volume includes the first five debates in the series and features twenty leading thinkers and doers arguing for or against provocative resolutions that address pressing public policy concerns, such as the future of global security, the implications of humanitarian intervention, the effectiveness of foreign aid, the threat of climate change, and the state of health care in Canada and the United States.

"By trying to highlight the most important issues at crucial moments in the global conversation, these debates not only profile the ideas and solutions of some of our brightest thinkers and doers, but crystallize public passion and knowledge, helping to tackle some global challenges confronting humankind."

——Peter Munk

houseofanansi.com/collections/munk-debates